D1278631

1. Make the produce manager of your favorite supermarket into your assistant kitchen chef. He will always give you the finest products he has available!

2. Purchase and use the high-quality baked breads, fresh pastas, and triple-washed vegetables you can find in every supermarket.

3. Save time and essential nutrients in one fell swoop! Wash but do not peel most fruits and potatoes.

4. Never underestimate your food processor's capabilities!

5. Always make enough to save some for later—then you'll know that a quick, healthy meal is as close as your freezer!

*One luxurious bubble bath*

*Access to most comfortable chair and favorite TV show*

*One half-hour massage (will need to recruit spouse, child, friend)*

*Time to recline and listen to a favorite CD (or at least one song)*

cut

6. Multi-task! Take advantage of the time you're waiting on the oven to get other things done!

7. The Crock Pot is the perfect assistant—it'll cook all day while you're busy, and it will never get stressed or irritable!

8. Make survival into a communal effort. It is not carved into stone that one person (you) should be both cook and bottle-washer.

9. Clean up your kitchen as you cook. Never consider cleanup to be only an after-meal chore.

10 Plan every aspect of your dinner parties so that you do not miss the festivities—the lazy cook will find recipes that can be made the day before the party.

COUPON

COUPON

COUPON

COUPON

# Cooking Vegetarian

# Cooking Vegetarian

Barbara Grunes

Macmillan • USA

With much love and pride, I would like to dedicate this book to my two handsome new grandsons, Ethan and Noah Kraus, and to my husband, Jerry, for his constant encouragement and patience.

Macmillan Publishing books may be purchased for business or sales promotional use. For information please write: Special Markets Department, Macmillan Publishing USA, 1633 Broadway, New York, NY 10019.

International Standard Book Number: 0-02863158-7
Library of Congress Catalog Card Number: 99-61469

01  00  99    8  7  6  5  4  3  2  1

Interpretation of the printing code: the rightmost number of the first series of numbers is the year of the book's printing; the rightmost number of the second series of numbers is the number of the book's printing. For example, a printing code of 99-1 shows that the first printing occurred in 1999.

Printed in the United States of America

Book Design: Madhouse Studios

Page creation by Heather Pope and Ellen Considine

# You Don't Have to Feel Guilty Anymore!

## IT'S O.K. TO DO IT *THE LAZY WAY!*

It seems every time we turn around, we're given more responsibility, more information to absorb, more places we need to go, and more numbers, dates, and names to remember. Both our bodies and our minds are already on overload. And we know what happens next—cleaning the house, balancing the checkbook, and cooking dinner get put off until "tomorrow" and eventually fall by the wayside.

So let's be frank—we're all starting to feel a bit guilty about the dirty laundry, stacks of ATM slips, and Chinese takeout. Just thinking about tackling those terrible tasks makes you exhausted, right? If only there were an easy, effortless way to get this stuff done! (And done right!)

There is—*The Lazy Way*! By providing the pain-free way to do something—including tons of shortcuts and time-saving tips, as well as lists of all the stuff you'll ever need to get it done efficiently—*The Lazy Way* series cuts through all of the time-wasting thought processes and laborious exercises. You'll discover the secrets of those who have figured out *The Lazy Way*. You'll get things done in half the time it takes the average person—and then you will sit back and smugly consider those poor suckers who haven't discovered *The Lazy Way* yet. With *The Lazy Way,* you'll learn how to put in minimal effort and get maximum results so you can devote your attention and energy to the pleasures in life!

## THE LAZY WAY PROMISE

Everyone on *The Lazy Way* staff promises that, if you adopt *The Lazy Way* philosophy, you'll never break a sweat, you'll barely lift a finger, you won't put strain on your brain, and you'll have plenty of time to put up your feet. We guarantee you will find that these activities are no longer hardships, since you're doing them *The Lazy Way*. We also firmly support taking breaks and encourage rewarding yourself (we even offer our suggestions in each book!). With *The Lazy Way*, the only thing you'll be overwhelmed by is all of your newfound free time!

## THE LAZY WAY SPECIAL FEATURES

Every book in our series features the following sidebars in the margins, all designed to save you time and aggravation down the road.

- **"Quick 'n' Painless"**—shortcuts that get the job done fast.
- **"You'll Thank Yourself Later"**—advice that saves time down the road.
- **"A Complete Waste of Time"**—warnings that spare countless headaches and squandered hours.
- **"If You're So Inclined"**—optional tips for moments of inspired added effort.
- **"The Lazy Way"**—rewards to make the task more pleasurable.

If you've either decided to give up altogether or have taken a strong interest in the subject, you'll find information on hiring outside help with "How to Get Someone Else to Do It" as well as further reading recommendations in "If You Want to Learn More, Read These." In addition, there's an only-what-you-need-to-know glossary of terms and product names ("If You Don't Know What It Means/Does, Look Here") as well as "It's Time for Your Reward"—fun and relaxing ways to treat yourself for a job well done.

With *The Lazy Way* series, you'll find that getting the job done has never been so painless!

| | |
|---|---|
| **Series Editor** | **Managing Editor** |
| Amy Gordon | Robert Shuman |

*[signature: Amy Gordon]*      *[signature: Bob Shuman]*

| | |
|---|---|
| **Editorial Director** | **Development Editor** |
| Gary Krebs | Alana J. Morgan |

*[signature: Gary Krebs]*      *[signature: Alana Morgan]*

**Production Editor**
Christy Wagner

*[signature: christy wagner]*

**Director of Creative Services**
Michele Laseau

*[signature: Michele Laseau]*

**Cover Designer**
Michael Freeland

*[signature: Michael J. Freeland]*

# What's in This Book

## MORE LAZY STUFF

# No Time to Spare? Just Because You're Busy, That Doesn't Mean You Can't Eat Healthy!

I grew up once upon a time when it was absolutely expected that there would be meat and potatoes on the table. It was a different, more regimented era, and people possessed more traditional—shall we say—conformist culinary values.

Later I was beleaguered by life's really important matters, like trying to figure out my psychotic boss or rushing the clothes to the cleaners so that the sales presentation would not have to be done in cutoffs and a T-shirt. My cooking time usually involved popping hot dogs into boiling water or flopping hastily formed hamburger patties into a frying pan. Then came the realization that the family was becoming a group of greasy "beef babies," and we were actually endangering our health.

All the same, I was under the ironclad impression that healthy cooking required a 30-hour day and an 8-day week. I believed that vegetarian cooking was the realm of the vastly rich and the eminently thin. A land filled with those strange people who actually had the time and energy to make daily trips to farmers' markets or exotic fat-off ports where they could obtain fresh, impossible-to-pronounce vegetables and fruits. A kingdom of folks who grew organic grains in penthouse gardens and who communed mystically with guru culinary experts.

Two events changed my personal life and, ironically, truly simplified it. First, my husband was diagnosed as a diabetic, and second, as a result, I revised my culinary philosophy and wrote my first vegetarian cookbook. The entire family and my dinner guests became vegetarian-lovers over time, and I became a vegetarian advocate. Most interestingly, it was stunning to note the variety of vegetarian dishes and meals, and with a little forethought, the ease of their preparation.

So relax and read further. Vegetarian cooking will be not only a healthy mind- and body-altering experience, but also an experience that will be an easy, time-and-labor-saving process, and fun. Finally, unless you spill the beans, so to speak, your family and guests will never again feel the need to ask, "Where's the beef?"

In this book, you will read about shopping and storing techniques, labor-saving ways, and family satisfaction-tested vegetarian cooking methods that I have garnered during the last 10 years. I will share a myriad of incredibly lazy-styled, taste-bud-bursting vegetarian recipes for breakfasts, lunches, dinners, appetizers, midday and midnight snacks, grill parties, holiday feasts, and full-course gourmet dinner parties that will leave everyone at your table beaming sublimely and hoping that the digestive process will soon make it possible to take on an additional portion.

This book is for everyone who desires a wonderful, healthy, vegetarian meal, obtained in the most effortless and economical way. You can enjoy vegetarian food one or two or three times a week, you can be a complete vegetarian, or you can adapt some of these lazy techniques to other varieties of vegetarianism. You will find panic-free instructions for spur-of-the-moment vegetarian party menus and lazy-style but perfect dishes suitable for a pizza party or a gourmet dinner.

In order to help you garner the manifold benefits of this book in the simplest and most efficient manner, I have presented essential dos and don'ts for food preparation, cooking, and presentation. You will find that the recipes are designed to avoid the classic, "I'd love to prepare this meal, but just look at the 36-page recipe," and presented to allow you the highest degree of "lazy," easy preparation and comfort. These will all add up to a new degree of culinary confidence.

The sidebars in this book will provide quick and agony-proof ways to perform tasks, suggest fun projects to try, advise you on plan-ahead strategies to make life easier, avoid potential disasters, and share ideas for rewarding yourself, family, and guests with never-ending scrumptious, happy, and healthy vegetarian eating. I've also included some important nutrition information in Appendix F from the U.S. Department of Agriculture's Food Guide Pyramid to an explanation of what a serving size means to you. So relax and read on, healthy eating is just a page turn away!

## THANK YOU . . .

I would like to acknowledge and thank: David Marion for his tireless effort and encouragement; Virginia van Vynck for her friendship and help; Amy Gordon, Series Editor and leader, for her enthusiasm in this project; Alana Morgan, Development Editor, for her hard work and patience; and Martha Castelman for her dedication and loyalty.

## Part 1

# Managing the Marketplace

## Are You Too Lazy to Read Managing the Marketplace?

**1** Your kitchen closely resembles Julia Child's kitchen—just after a tornado has passed through. ☐ yes ☐ no

**2** Your kitchen makes Mother Hubbard's look overstocked. ☐ yes ☐ no

**3** The last time you had handily available the correct spices, canned goods, grains, and dry goods required for a recipe that you decided to throw together was, well, never. ☐ yes ☐ no

# Getting Ready but Staying Steady: The Vegetarian Kitchen

**A**be Lincoln once said, "If I had just 10 hours to chop down a tree, I'd spend the first seven sharpening my ax." The main difference between a laborious, frustrating cooking process and an easy, pleasurable one is preparation. If your pantry, cabinets, and refrigerator are stocked properly, your vegetarian meals will not only be easy to prepare, but also wonderful to eat.

Shopping can be like fighting monsters in a terribly confused and disturbing dream, but it need not be. Often, the real difference between the constantly perturbed, average cook and the relaxed, good cook is the ability to shop well.

To wrap the skill of shopping into a nutshell, it means being ready to shop, having already thought about the shopping mission rather than just going shopping. These ideas should make you into an instant smart shopper.

## DON'T SHOP 'TIL YOU DROP

There's no need for multiple trips to the store or coming home with everything but what you really need! Follow these simple guidelines to make your shopping excursions efficient:

- Your culinary bible is your shopping list. Always remember the old Boy Scout motto: Be prepared.

- Keep an ongoing monthly list, adding (or deleting) items as the need for them arises.

- Always think, think, think (it's easier than doing) about your shopping needs before you go.

- Narrow your shopping list to what you will use. Good, relaxed cooks actually use a small variety of foodstuffs, but they use those items over and over again.

- Shop only at predetermined intervals. Avoid like the plague the daily rush to the store for some item you need at the moment.

- Plan ahead for special events and special needs— house guests, parties, club luncheons, special family occasions, holidays, and even Sunday meals. Add special-need goods to your monthly shopping list and highlight them.

- Choose a time of day to shop and try to stick to that time. If you have planned ahead and shop at regular intervals, this should be easy. Pick a time of day when the market is most like a monastery. This time could be late at night when you get to know the third-shift stocking help on a first-name basis.

- Use the phone book, both for finding convenient supermarkets and for locating specialty, ethnic, and fresh-produce markets.

- For goodness sake, use delivery services if they're available! The phone book and your computer will open a world of convenience and ease in this matter. Why drive, park, shop, stand in line, load, and unload supplies when a delivery can bring virtually everything you need directly to your door—sometimes within the hour?

- Find and frequent co-ops, organic, and ethnic markets, and always buy in bulk when you can.

- On the other hand, buy only small amounts of lesser-used foods. Do you honestly need two pounds of black sesame seeds?

- Familiarize yourself with the markets you frequent. Plan a route through the store that is most convenient and simple. You should be able to organize your shopping list into a game plan that will carry you through the market as if on a magic carpet.

- Shop methodically. Avoid being distracted by attractive displays and sample tables. Avoid lengthy market conversations; "It's good to see you, Thelma; I'll call you later" is enough.

- Always eat something—at least a snack—before you go shopping. Guess why.

YOU'LL THANK YOURSELF LATER

**If you're short of cupboard space, the wall between the cabinets and countertop is a great place to put spice racks, towel-bars, hooks for utensils, etc.**

Congratulations! You've made it so you can find anything in your kitchen whenever you need it! Treat yourself to a night out at the movies!

*The Lazy Way*

# IF YOU CAN'T FIND IT, YOU AIN'T GOT IT!

I assume that you spend frustrating time nosing around your cabinets, looking for required ingredients. Let's end that never-ending cycle right now. You must be able to instantly see, identify, and grab the items you need in any cooking endeavor. Repeat after me: "Forever more, I will place all foodstuffs in airtight glass jars for easy visual identification." The following storage items are essential and are the secret to making your kitchen easy to manage:

- Mason jars or other glass or crystal-clear plastic containers in various sizes. These items are the basis for creating a quick and simple ingredient discovery method.
- A revolving (or huge), visible spice rack with neatly and clearly labeled bottles. 'Nuff said.
- A bread box.
- A cabinet and pantry shelf ordering system of light plywood or plastic dividers. Devise your own system, but to avoid a Fibber McGee's closet scenario, do something and stick with it.

## I GOT IT! I GOT IT!

The average American kitchen contains a mishmash of goods—too much of everything except what you need at the given moment, too little of the basics of cooking to be "ready to cook," and far too much disorganization to be useful. Be candid: Don't you have some exotic spices or canned goods or ethnic foods that still retain their original seal? And don't you have a mostly empty bag of whole-wheat flour that should have been replenished last month? So, to begin, compare the following lists with what you currently have on hand and make your shopping list accordingly. The following staples are a must in the vegetarian kitchen:

- **Vegetable stock.** This is one of the mainstays of vegetarian cooking, and you should always keep either homemade, canned, granular, frozen, or cubed vegetable stock on hand. Recipes for several varieties of vegetable stock are included in this book. When you need vegetable stock for a recipe, which you will frequently, you have only to boil water, add dried stock, and bingo!

- **All-purpose, unbleached, and whole-wheat flours.** Fortunately, for your convenience, most commercial flour has been presifted, but you should still stir it a bit before spooning into a measuring cup. Whole-wheat flour is more flavorful and contains wheat germ and bran, making it more nutritious and higher in fiber than white flour.

- **Quinoa.** Never heard of it? Don't feel lonely—trust me, it's a keeper. Quinoa is an ancient South American grain that is relatively new to the American market. A complete protein because it contains all nine of the essential amino acids, it is rich in vitamins and minerals. Quinoa can be a substitute for rice, as a side dish, and as part of many entrees, soups, and salads. If you can't find quinoa

**IF YOU'RE SO INCLINED**

A vegan does not eat or use any animal products, including dairy selections or eggs. This also includes things such as leather or wool clothing, and they would also never purchase a product tested on animals. Some vegans expand this practice to not eating honey or yeast products.

in your local supermarket, check the local health food store.

- **Oils—olive oil.** Keep things simple: Use Italian or Greek virgin olive oil for cooking and extra virgin olive oil for salads. Another good cooking oil is canola oil, which is lower in saturated fat than any other vegetable oil and is a good source of mono-unsaturated fat and omega-3 fatty acids.

- **Spices.** Believe it or not, they do go stale, so buy spices in small amounts and restock often. It's a good idea to have the following spices on hand:

  - Basil
  - Bay leaves—but always remove bay leaves from food before serving time
  - Curry powder
  - Dill
  - Fennel seeds
  - Garlic powder
  - Ground allspice
  - Ground cinnamon
  - Ground cumin or cumin seeds
  - Ground nutmeg
  - Lemon grass
  - Marjoram
  - Mint
  - Oregano
  - Paprika

- Parsley

- Pepper: black, white, and red pepper flakes

- Powdered ginger

- Rosemary

- Sage

- Tarragon

- Thyme

- **Condiments.** Spicy, salty, or piquant relishes, sauces, and spice mixtures add zing and zest to many vegetarian dishes, producing complementary or contrasting tastes.

  - **Ketchup.** Used both as an ingredient and as a sauce, ketchup is currently undergoing a long-overdue metamorphosis; flavored ketchups have begun to enter the market in a steady stream.

  - **Prepared mustard.** Try stone-ground mustard, dijon, or sweet-and-sour mustard. Mustards are great with many foods. Mix hot and/or flavored mustards and lemon juice into salads for a lazy and healthful dressing.

  - **Salsa.** Its popularity knows no end . . . go for it!

  - **Mayonnaise.** Regular or light—your choice!

  - **Pesto.** I recommend that you use pesto sauce on most everything. Be creative! Try it on salads or pizza as well as on pasta. Use a light hand if you're timid and a heavy one if you're like me.

**IF YOU'RE SO INCLINED**

Make your own flavored mustards. It's very simple: Blend horseradish, hot sauce, wine, or your favorite spices into prepared mustard to create your own personalized "brands." If you create a perfect mustard, name it, bottle it, label it, and give it to friends as a gift.

- **Soy sauce.** This flavoring sauce is made from fermented soybeans and wheat. It is an essential ingredient in many Asian dishes.

- **Hoisin sauce.** This is a sweet and spicy, soybean-based Asian sauce. It has continued to be the favorite flavoring sauce of my youngest daughter—Doctor Dorothy. As a child she would use it on all kinds of food, including pasta.

- **Tabasco or other hot sauces.** A small amount of hot sauce can lend its zing to almost any bland dish. Use at your own discretion.

- **Vinegar.** Vinegar is used in pickling, canning, and in small amounts for flavoring salads and dressings.

  - **Balsamic vinegar.** This has an intense yet somewhat sweet and tart flavor. It's wonderful on salads.

  - **Wine vinegar.** This is a mild-tasting vinegar, good for marinades, sauces, and salad dressings.

  - **Cider vinegar.** This has a tart and fruity flavor. It is made from apples and is good in salad dressings.

  - **Rice vinegar.** This has a sharp, slightly mellow taste. Use it on salads.

  - **Fruit vinegars.** These are made from cider vinegar or white-wine vinegar with the addition of a small amount of fruit such as cranberries, raspberries, or oranges. It

makes a fine dressing for salad, but you can also drizzle it on some grilled foods, such as grilled chicken—for you less-strict vegetarians—or even splash on fruit.

- **Sweeteners.** These help both flavor and brown foods, and in some cases, can replace some of the fat.

  - Dark and light brown sugar
  - Granulated sugar
  - Fruit-based purees
  - Honey
  - Malt syrup
  - Maple syrup
  - Rice syrup

- **Dried fruit and preserves.** Dried fruits make perfect snack foods and preserves on bread, or when mixed with nonfat yogurt make superior dessert substitutes. Don't hesitate to purchase some of the more offbeat dried fruits, such as papaya or kiwi, to provide variety.

  - Currants, dark or golden raisins
  - Dates
  - Figs
  - Assorted dried fruits—apricots, apples, or other fruits of your choice

- **Dried (or canned) beans.** Packed with protein, fiber, vitamins, and minerals, legumes are important and basic in a vegetarian diet. Choose the beans that

Congratulations! You've made a simply lazy, yet amazingly delicious, dessert with some fresh fruit and a dash of fruit vinegar! Reward yourself with a massage!

The Lazy Way

Purchase a food drier and dry your own fruits. The only effort involved is slicing your fruits, which can be done in the food processor, and then turning on the drier. Then you're free to go about your vocation, avocation, and normal activities while the fruit dries for 24 hours. Dried fruits can be reconstituted in water, eaten out of hand, or used in baking.

your family likes best then experiment with other beans they might enjoy. Introduce a new bean occasionally (but announce it only after everyone has cleaned his plate!). Don't forget canned refried beans (use the low-fat, vegetarian versions).

- **Grains.** Grains are the building blocks of any nutritious diet. They supply abundant amounts of **complex carbohydrates** (starches). The body burns both complex and **simple carbohydrates** (sugars) for fuel. Whole grains provide fiber and a wider range of nutrients, including thiamin (vitamin B-1), riboflavin (vitamin B-2), folate, chromium, magnesium, manganese, molybdenum, phosphorus, and potassium. Some grains are also rich in iron, calcium, or zinc.

  - Grains
    - Barley
    - Buckwheat
    - Bulgur
    - Corn
    - Couscous
    - Farina
    - Millet
    - Oats
    - Rice
    - Rye
    - Semolina
    - Wheat wild rice

- High-protein grains
    - Amaranth
    - Quinoa
    - Spelt
    - Teff

- **Pasta.** Where to start? With every succeeding year, pasta becomes increasingly more popular in American cooking. Because of an increased demand, a vast and varied assortment of pastas has become available in the marketplace. There are hundreds of types, shapes, sizes, textures, flavors, and colors of pasta. Dry pastas should be stored in airtight glass gars in a cool, dry place. It should be easy to visually identify the various pastas on your shelves in their containers. Despite what energetic food writers with massive amounts of time to kill may tell you, making your own pasta from scratch today is strictly for hobbyists and restaurant chefs. High-quality fresh pasta, often in flavors such as chili, herb, and beet, is now readily available at virtually every supermarket.

- **Rice and instant rice.** Both plain and brown rice come in an instant form, perfect for the lazy cook. Be sure always to cook an extra cup or two of rice and store it in the freezer for a quick meal. As an extra tip, rice that's been refrigerated for at least two days is the best option for making fried rice.

- **Nuts.** Nuts are essential for the vegetarian because they are rich in proteins that we would normally get from meats.

**IF YOU'RE SO INCLINED**

Some high-fiber foods you should know about: oat bran, oatmeal, cooked brown rice, whole-wheat flour, cooked legumes, all-bran cereal, fruits such as figs, apples, and oranges, and vegetables such as carrots and broccoli.

- Almonds
- Hazelnuts
- Peanuts
- Pecans
- Pine nuts
- Walnuts

- **Onions.** Both white or yellow.

- **Minced garlic.** Buy it in a jar, or try minced garlic and ginger together in a jar. What inventions!

- **Potatoes.** White, red, sweet, and boiling potatoes. Potatoes have correctly been called "the most versatile member of the vegetable family." Since potatoes can be kept successfully for up to a month if stored in a cool, dark, well-ventilated area, buy them by the bag. Sweet potatoes, of course, aren't potatoes (they're yams, which are a root plant), but they're usually sold alongside them.

- **Tomatoes.** Canned tomatoes, tomato sauce, and tomato paste. Canned tomatoes come in an amazing variety. I also suggest that you have a good supply of sliced and crushed tomatoes at all times. They are a great step-saver over whole, canned tomatoes, as they are already crushed and sliced.

- **Eggs.** Eggs are low in calories and a good source of protein, fat, vitamins, minerals, calcium, iron, vitamins A and D, and riboflavin. Cholesterol is found in eggs, so some of us need to use eggs in moderation. Use large eggs unless otherwise specified in a recipe, and always store them in the refrigerator. Don't

*QUICK* 🔘 *PAINLESS*

Substitute canola blend oil when possible if you are concerned about your cholesterol.

forget that egg substitutes are also available. If you decide to use substitutes, remember this tip: A $\frac{1}{4}$ cup egg substitute equals 1 egg.

- **Cheese.** Cheese comes in categories: Hard cheeses such as Romano, Paramigiano, and Asagio; semi-firm cheeses such as cheddar, Emmentaler, and Gloucester; veined cheeses such as blue cheese, Gorgonzola, and Stilton; semi-soft cheeses such as Gouda and Fontina; and soft cheeses such as Brie and Camembert. There are dozens and dozens of cheeses from which to choose. These are only a few of my favorites.

## SEARCHING FOR MR. RIGHT, OR GETTING TO KNOW THE PRODUCE MANAGER

In today's hectic, nonpersonal world, it's hard to get to know your neighbors, let alone the produce managers at the supermarkets and specialty markets where you shop. However, in the interests of lazy vegetarian cooking, I must suggest that a little friendliness, naiveté, and respect can be the keys to lazy, yet incredibly successful, fresh-food shopping. You must either put yourself in the hands of a superior produce manager at the best super-market produce department you can find or in the hands of the owner/manager of a year-round fruit and veg-etable specialty market, or better yet, in the hands of both. Candidly admit your lack of expertise in selecting, storing, and using fresh fruits and vegetables, and they'll surely come to your aid.

Congratulations! You've put together a grocery list your arteries will be proud of! Give yourself a break and kick back with a good book!

The Lazy Way

No one will be able to resist this appeal, and if you are a good customer and a good friend, you soon may find that the produce manager is your most valuable friend.

# Getting Time on Your Side

| | The Old Way | The Lazy Way |
|---|---|---|
| Getting the groceries | Many trips, every week | One trip, once a week |
| Putting together a shopping list | Oops! | Already done! |
| Finding the stuff in your kitchen | Darn! I could have sworn I had that! | Right on the shelf marked "Spices" |
| Getting in and out of the market | Hours | 30 minutes |
| Finding fresh produce | Darn! | Every time (it's easy when you've got a produce manager in your corner!) |

# Taming the Technology

**S**ometimes when things are going well for me and I'm happy and upbeat, I occasionally feel a need for a dose of equilibrium. So I let my mind wander to previous times—to medieval castle kitchens, to one-room adobe huts with outdoor cooking fires, to pioneer women trekking across the plains with their kitchen facilities on wheels. Then I sit with my head in my hands until the cold sweats pass, and I thank the powers that be for the luxuries of our modern age.

Here's the culinary good news: You don't need an elaborate, high-tech, polished stainless-steel kitchen to be either a good or a lazy cook! In fact, for most kitchens, especially those of time-stressed cooks, simplicity is a great and real asset to ease and convenience.

The culinary bad news: The market is so flooded with new labor-saving kitchen devices and appliances that not only does it take time, study, and knowledge—in short, work—to keep up with this developing market, but also the willpower to avoid overfilling your kitchen with all of this fancy, newfangled paraphernalia.

Back to the good news: In this chapter I will simplify the kitchen equipment selection by providing you with a list of basic equipment that will make your vegetarian cooking endeavors as lazy and simple—and as totally automated—as possible.

As I have mentioned earlier, my own kitchen has been radically simplified in recent years to my tremendous advantage. The following appliances, electric and battery-powered devices, and hand tools are indispensable and will kick the dickens out of hard work and long preparation.

## TURN ON THE POWER, TURN OFF THE EFFORT

We've all been taking advantage of the amazing power of electricity for ages now, but often we tend to neglect the great bonuses of appliances. Don't turn your back on these little helpers!

### The Food Processor

These incredibly versatile machines offer a fairly mind-boggling variety of features, including the ability to blend, chop, shred, slice, mince, grate, beat, mix, puree, grind, and optionally knead. The food processor is the single most valuable tool in the lazy vegetarian cook's kitchen.

The time- and effort-saving potential of a food processor cannot be overemphasized. I would encourage you to plan every recipe with the food processor in mind. Actually, other than literally cooking a dish, there are few chores that cannot be entrusted to your trusty food processor. Leave it on the counter, ready to use.

If you already own a food processor, great! You're a step ahead of the game! If not, make sure the quality and capability of the processor is your primary concern when purchasing one. Buy the best processor you can afford but also one that fits your family needs—the medium size is usually best, but if you only tend to use your processor for small amounts of food, then a smaller size should suit you perfectly. Processors that come with a powerful motor and high-quality, wear-resistant, and multipurpose accessories are well worth their cost. Other accessories, such as julienne, thin, and other specialty blades can add convenience, but you should remember that you will use your processor for basic tasks 99 percent of the time. The smaller processors are also good tools when it comes to chopping and mincing small amounts of food such as garlic or ginger.

## More Electric Efficiency for Your Kitchen!

While the food processor is definitely the star player, don't overlook these other appliances. They are the perfect addition to the lazy kitchen, and you'll wonder how you ever lived without them before!

- **Blender.** This is the perfect tool if you are performing small, quick-cooking tasks. Setup and cleanup of the blender are extremely easy.

- **Electric Crock Pot.** This tool is truly the lazy person's wheel. Place the recipe ingredients into the Crock Pot in the morning and spend the day at work, at

QUICK PAINLESS

I used to place candy, chips, and salted nuts all over my house as the default snacks for visitors. Now I use my food processor to slice up fresh fruits, such as apples and pears, and vegetables, such as radishes, green onions, and cauliflower, on the spur of moment and provide minced goody bowls whenever we have guests.

the beach, or take a nap while the meal prepares itself, subtly combining flavors and tenderizing the most rugged foods.

- **Electric can opener.** The big question here is "Why?" Why look for a manual can opener every time in a big drawer full of kitchen utensils? Why risk cutting off a fingertip every time you open a can? Why fight with the twisted tin remnants of every can? Why get halfway around the can only to have the opener come off its route? Why, why, why? Stop asking why and see the one great truth: An electric can opener is the perfect solution for speed, convenience, and safety.

- **Electric vegetable/rice steamers.** These little helpers are great for all of you lazy cooks out there! Just dump in the rice, set the timer, and you're all set. Some versions come with sets of bowls and layers so you can steam your rice and vegetables all at once, as well as a place for herbs and spices so you can infuse your food with some great flavor. There's even rumor of a model that can also be used as an ice-cream maker (who knew?)!

## YES, IT'S MANUAL, BUT YOU DON'T NEED A MANUAL TO RUN IT

There are still some classic kitchen tools that have stood the test of time and have been voted by yours truly as absolutely indispensable.

YOU'LL THANK YOURSELF LATER

If you are using your processor to accomplish multiple tasks during the preparation of a recipe or meal, you can avoid having to clean the bowl after each use by processing the dry foods first and then the wet foods. And here's another tip: Process the strongest foods, like onions and leeks, after you have processed the less potent foods.

## The Big- and Medium-Sized, Easy Hide-a-Way Helpers

You may not need them all the time, but you'll be glad you have them when you do. Some things you just don't need to automate to achieve perfection!

### Full Steam Ahead! Steamer Baskets and Bamboo Steamers

A steamer basket is a metal devise, usually with collapsible sides and vent holes, designed to fit inside pots. Steamer baskets are absolutely perfect for steaming vegetables because they let you retain much more of the vegetables' nutrition than you can with boiling.

Bamboo steamers are made to fit inside an electric or stove-top wok. They can be found in cookware stores and in some Asian markets. Bamboo steamers are great, not only because they are attractive kitchen items, but also because they provide a slow, continuous flow of steam to the vegetables, rather than bombarding them with the high concentration of moisture that metal steamer baskets do.

### Life Can Be a Cake-Wok!

Wok, don't run, in the kitchen, because a wok will add simplicity as well as zest and fun to your vegetarian cooking repertoire. A wok is a perfectly designed frying pan, usually made of spun steel, which conducts the heat through all areas of the metal. You can create huge, party-sized meals using your wok or cook for one. This versatility makes wok cooking both a pleasure and a breeze! If you don't have a wok, and aren't really up to

QUICK ⬤ PAINLESS

You can keep flavored, steamed vegetables fresh for a few days if you store them in the refrigerator in airtight, plastic bags. You can also puree these vegetables in your processor or blender.

going out and buying one now, you can stir-fry in a large skillet, but the wok is really the best way to go with this one!

### Open Sesame! It's Easy with a Jar Opener!

Save the hands and macho self-image of all male members of your family. Attach a jar opener to the underside of one of your cabinets, and you will never regret it. These incredibly simple devices are worth their weight in gold, Epsom salts, and aspirin.

## Little, Powerful Guys, Worth Twice Their Weight in Work

Don't forget, sometimes the best things come in small packages! These tools are required for the lazy cook!

### Everyone's Gotta Chop!

Don't skimp on your kitchen knives! You don't need to have every type and size of knife that was ever made; a few good knives will go a long way. I find that my medium-sized, serrated knife gets a lot of use. A vegetable paring knife is another good investment that you shouldn't do without. Be sure to include one large and one medium knife in your slicing and dicing arsenal. Make sure you know how to take advantage of these invaluable assistants, and keep your knives sharp (they will like it and so will you!). But do be careful to keep them out of the reach of small children.

### Maximize the Power of the Fruit!

Get yourself a citrus reamer or juicer. I love my wooden reamer and use it for fresh juice. Once you start using

YOU'LL THANK YOURSELF LATER

Bok choy is one of the best vegetable sources of absorbable calcium.

this tool, you'll soon wonder why you ever bothered with bottled lemon juice.

## Lilliputian Tools to the Rescue!

Never underestimate the value of a few well-chosen weapons in your cooking arsenal. These items may be small, but they are absolutely indispensable!

YOU'LL THANK YOURSELF LATER

**Purchase oranges and grapefruits in bulk when they are freshest and cheapest. Juice a batch of each daily, keep the fresh juice in the refrigerator in clear containers, and watch your family members drink it down.**

- **Kitchen scissors.** I have a pair of kitchen scissors— that is, a pair of scissors reserved for use in the kitchen—which are in constant use, and I would be lost without them.

- **Colander and/or salad spinner.** You will never be sorry to have either or both of these items. A colander is necessary if you cook with pasta, and salad spinners deliver crisper, fresher-tasting greens.

- **Wire whisk.** A great tool for creating smooth sauces when the pot is on the stove.

- **Kitchen timer.** Indispensable for a lazy cook. Be sure to get a timer with a loud alarm so that it will awaken you from your nap when the lazy meal preparation is complete and it's time for the hard work to begin: dining.

- **Kitchen scale.** Hey, sometimes the eyeball method works great, and it's easy, but a scale will save you many frustrating minutes of mental and paperwork computation.

- **Big glass measuring cup.** Like the big rock candy mountain in Candy Land, the big glass measuring cup is sweet. It will handle almost any measuring job

in one step, and you can see the contents as you measure—what more could you ask for?

- **Nonstick pots and pans.** Not only are they great for cooking and a easy cleanup, nonstick also requires far less oil or spray.

- **Nonstick stirring utensils and spatula.** They won't scratch your nonstick pots and pans, and they're easier to clean. These are definitely a must have!

- **A fine set of pot holders.** Keep them in a very handy place or you'll be reaching for the dish towel and burning yourself on the cooking element.

## WOULDN'T IT BE LOVERLY?

Sure, the following items are luxuries in the kitchen, and certainly not essential, but they're very handy, and they will save you much time and reward you with wonderfully edible products. Remember, though, if your kitchen is compact, cluttering it with equipment will not save you time in the long run; it will complicate your life in many ways.

- **Convection oven.** In a convection oven, a fan circulates the air from above and below and cooks food faster, more thoroughly, and more evenly. The use of a convection oven is an old chef's secret in commercial kitchens. Many of the new stoves come with either a regular and/or a convection oven. There are also many good counter-top convection ovens.

- **Food drier.** Creates great, yummy, good-for-you products.

- **Bread maker.** The new generation of bread makers are cheap, efficient, and they create fabulous products most of the time. However, fresh-baked bread of every imaginable type is so readily available today that it's probably more convenient and time-efficient to purchase fresh bread than to make it. If you do decide you need a bread maker, make sure it has a delayed-start timer, a dough cycle, and a whole-wheat cycle.

- **Electric corer/peeler.** They make everything these days, don't they? If you have the capital and a place to put one, go for it. Every minute saved is a minute for you to do what you want to do rather than what you need to do or have to do.

- **Microwave oven.** Microwave ovens have become so prevalent in American kitchens that I should probably include this item on the indispensable list. However, my microwave is used much less frequently than my stove. I'm sure that everyone will agree that a microwave is undeniably a time-saving device.

- **Stove-top grill.** This is a neat, inexpensive device that allows you to bring summer into your kitchen during the storms of winter. The grill fits directly over one or two of your stove burners. You can still achieve the grilled look—with those cool sear marks—if not always the grilled taste.

- **Cordless phone.** Whistle while you work. Kill two birds with one stone. Need I say more?

**YOU'LL THANK YOURSELF LATER**

Prioritize your movements from appliance to appliance. If you have worn a path in the kitchen floor linoleum, you know that you do not have your appliances positioned correctly. Move the appliances to the right places for your personal kitchen routine. Remember that old saying, "A step in time saves nine."

Right now, this minute, formulate a kitchen space plan and organize your appliances and wall racks to afford you the greatest amount of convenience and step-saving possible. Eliminate every single piece of clutter from your counter space. Decorative items have their place—out of the way somewhere— preferably on the walls where they can be seen and not heard.

■ **Headset phone.** If you're super serious about talking and cooking, and spend enough time in the kitchen to warrant it, you might even think about getting yourself a headset phone that you can clip to your belt. Look ma! No hands!

# Getting Time on Your Side

|  | The Old Way | The Lazy Way |
|---|---|---|
| Chopping vegetables | 10 minutes | 2 seconds |
| Standing over a stew | All day | Never again! |
| Breaking your hands every time you open a jar | All the time | Never again! |
| Scraping the remains of dinner off your pots and pans | Hours | Never again! |
| Walking back and forth across the kitchen as you cook | Hours | Don't need to (you've created a kitchen that suits your lazy style!) |
| Kneading dough | 45 minutes | 5 minutes |

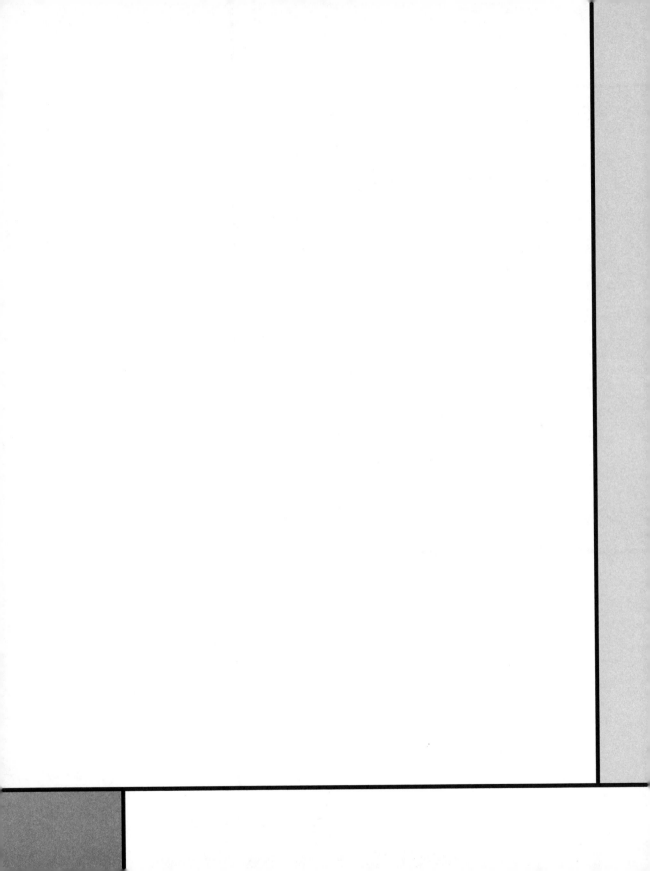

## Part 2

# It's Your Secret: Prepackaged Foods and Other Wondrous Innovations

### Are You Too Lazy to Read It's Your Secret: Prepackaged Foods and Other Wondrous Innovations?

**1** You feel that the easiest way to clean a kitchen is to burn down the house. ☐ yes ☐ no

**2** Nine of the 10 preprogrammed, automatic-dial numbers on your telephone are to pizza places. ☐ yes ☐ no

**3** Your freezer storage plan for leftovers and prepared foods looks like those 10,000-year-old Siberian frozen mammoth finds you read about in *National Geographic*. ☐ yes ☐ no

# Using Your Head, Not Your Hands

**H**ey, why reinvent the wheel? Whenever possible, use prepackaged, prepared foods to simplify vegetarian cooking. In an ideal world, all vegetarian recipes would be prepared from scratch, using the finest, freshest ingredients and large doses of loving care without worrying about time in the pursuit of a higher goal. But for the lazy cook, safe, healthy, and tasty dishes can be produced on a continual basis without expending half the time, energy, and usual frustration that gourmet cooking requires.

To provide shortcuts to good, simple, vegetarian cooking, here are some shopping hints for foods that should allow cooking ease and dispatch. Basically, it boils down to this: fresh, high-quality vegetarian ingredients usually need less time and effort, and they always taste better.

The upside is that the quality and availability of processed and prepackaged foods have exploded in recent years. Brand-name food manufacturers have discovered and appreciated the growing demand for products that are fresh, easy to

**Check out the protein (meat) alternatives that are available in your area. Tofu dogs, tempeh, vegetable burgers, and seitan are high-protein products.**

prepare, and come in meal-sized packages. A dazzling array of these products are now available, minced, diced, pureed, stewed, and simply or exotically preflavored.

By now, you should have obtained the basic staples for the kitchen, pantry, refrigerator, and freezer. You should have developed a plan for palming off your fresh fruit and vegetable decisions on your friendly produce manager. Now consider how to use your head rather than your hands in the modern, lazy, vegetarian kitchen. But remember, from this point onward, it's our secret.

## REAP THE MODERN HORN OF PLENTY

Always use good vegetarian products from your supermarket when those products can save you time and energy. Let the food manufacturers do these labor-intensive chores for you:

- Selecting and sectioning meal-sized portions
- Chopping, dicing, and mincing
- Precooking many foods
- Flavoring foods, especially by sautéing, mixing, rubbing, etc.

However, be sure to keep the manufacturers honest by:

- Visually inspecting visible ingredients
- Checking "sell by" and/or "use by" dates stamped on products
- Reading manufacturer information on products for cooking instructions, complementary foods, etc.

- Finding and asking informed employees any questions you might have about new products

## THE SUPERMARKET: A GARDEN OF EDEN FOR READY USE

It wasn't so long ago when any self-respecting kitchen cook shuddered at the mere mention of canned or processed foods. Sure, canned foods had some problems. They were hopelessly bland and usually incredibly salty.

Today, however, things have changed radically for the better. Food manufacturers have made fantastic strides at producing high-quality processed canned, frozen, dried, and prepackaged fresh foods that taste great. Have you seen all the processed foods in beautiful clear glass jars? Sales of these immensely convenient and simple-to-use foods have skyrocketed.

It should be the goal of the lazy cook to take advantage of this world of high-quality processed and prepackaged foods.

### Prepackaged Fresh Is Perfection

For the modern, time-constrained cook, prepackaged fresh foods must rate right up there with the invention of the wheel and the discovery of fire as a cooking aid. There is no better way to save time and effort while retaining the highest quality of ingredients than to purchase these wonderful products:

- **Packaged fresh vegetables.** These newly available products are a treat. They are invariably fresh; usually triple washed; shredded, sliced, or torn; mixed

QUICK ☺ PAINLESS

Spend some time at the service counter at your favorite supermarket. Here you can obtain a complete map of the store, specifying items by category and aisle, and a list of special services offered, including store policies concerning special orders and custom-preparation of foods for individual clients.

when appropriate; attractively presented; and ready to use. Here are just a few examples:

- Broccoli and cauliflower
- Broccoli coleslaw
- Creamy garlic Caesar
- Iceberg, romaine, leaf lettuce, radicchio, and frisee combinations
- Iceberg, romaine, red cabbage, carrot, and radish combinations
- Leaf lettuce, curly endive, and carrot combinations
- Oriental stir-fry vegetable mixes
- Romaine lettuce
- Shredded lettuce
- Sliced celery
- Sliced mushrooms
- Sliced or shredded carrots
- Snap peas
- Spinach

- **Herbs and spices.** A wide variety of herbs and spices are vacuum-packed as fresh products and hold that freshness, at least until the stamped "sell by" or "use by" date. Buy these items in small amounts and replace them as needed rather than buying in a large amount because they will loose their flavor.

- **Fruits.** Many fruits and fruit combinations are washed, sliced, and packaged in airtight plastic on a

daily basis in the produce departments of super-markets.

- Cantaloupe
- Grapefruit
- Oranges
- Pineapple
- Watermelon

- **Pasta.** Fresh pastas, particularly vegetable- and cheese-filled tortellini and ravioli, are delicious and almost effortless to use. These fresh packaged pastas cook quickly and are usually sold with complimentary sauces.

- **Breads.** What can I say? I defy you to find some kind of wonderfully exotic bread that is not cooked and packaged daily everywhere across America in bakeries, delis, specialty stores, and supermarkets (except, maybe for very small towns). I would even venture to say that there are as many baguettes sold daily in the United States as in France.

- **Fresh refrigerated foccacia bread and tortillas.** These items should not be overlooked. There are flavored, fresh packaged tortillas and wraps, such as tomato and basil, jalapeño and cilantro, honey wheat, garden spinach and herb, garden spinach and vegetable, and southwestern chipotle chili.

## Prepared Means Preparation

So many fine prepared foods are now available that it would take a voluntary kitchen workaholic, a culinary

**A COMPLETE WASTE OF TIME**

The 3 Worst Things to Do with Fresh Prepackaged Fruits and Vegetables:

1. Purchase less than you really need to use for a meal.

2. Wash them again. These products are triple-washed before packaging.

3. Chop them. They are chopped and ready for instant use.

purist, or a cookbook author to forgo the cooking assistance provided by prepared foods.

## Make It Saucy!

When it comes to pasta sauce—no matter how culinarily energetic you may feel on certain rare occasions—for day-to-day cooking, why make your own? You could better spend the time, say, polishing your bowling ball. Consider the following prepared, bottled, and canned sauces as examples:

- Tomato
- Tomato and basil
- Tomato, onion, and garlic
- Tomato Parmesan
- Spicy tomato

That's a sampling of the tomato-based sauces, but don't limit your creativity to the red fruit! Here are some other great sauce ideas, just waiting to be poured over your favorite pasta:

- Grilled summer vegetable
- Mushroom and diced tomato
- Mushroom and green pepper
- Mushroom and ripe olives
- Mushroom Parmesan
- Roasted garlic Parmesan

## Dip It or Spread It! The Choice Is Yours!

Salsas, dips, and spreads, like prepared pasta sauces, come in a staggering variety of good, tasty, indispensable

Congratulations! You wowed your surprise dinner guests with a great-tasting pasta sauce! Now reward yourself with a bowl of fruit sorbet! (Also ready-made, but who's telling?)

The Lazy Way

complements to main dishes, appetizers, and midnight snacks. In the course of a year, you will save yourself a whole vacation's worth of time by using these prepared items.

### The Italian Staple: Garlic

Purchase minced or chopped garlic. It's much nicer to spend your energy merely taking off the jar lid and spooning out the prepared garlic than trying to mince an object which by its size, shape, and nature does not want to be minced. Minced garlic also comes paired together with minced ginger.

### The Meat of Vegetables: Potatoes

Some varieties, such as Russets and Yukon Golds, are available at the produce counter, already washed, sliced, diced, grated, and packaged, ready to deep-fry or put in a casserole. Frozen potatoes and vegetables are a joy to prepare, as are mashed potatoes. For that very lazy day, try a dried potato mix.

### Order It Dried!

Dried foods are a well-known commodity. Most vegetarian cooks have plenty of experience using dried pastas, rice, mushrooms, and beans. Take advantage of the following dried foods, as their use will save you many kitchen preparation steps.

■ **Mixed dried beans.** These complementary bean combinations will allow you to prepare many popular bean soups and salads with relative simplicity. Many of these mixed-bean packages are spiced or include packages of spice.

**IF YOU'RE SO**
*INCLINED*

To create a handy supply of frozen individualized meals for use when everyone's schedule requires a separate mealtime, boil a huge pot of pasta and heat a huge saucepan of sauce. Use whatever portions are necessary, whether they're for lunch or the evening meal, seal in plastic bags, and freeze. When you're ready to use those extra portions you can just toss them into the microwave!

■ **Flavored rice and pilaf mixes.** These make terrific side dishes, as well as great bases for entrees. Dried rice and bean combinations are also available. One terrific time-saver is the use of packaged dried rice with various vegetables or ethnic flavors. Try Cajun, Southwest, or Spanish rice.

■ **Dried soup mixes.** There is a dazzling array of delicious dried soups available today, both in individual servings and family sizes. These require only the addition of boiling water and several minutes to steep. Here are just a few examples:

   ■ Cantonese rice

   ■ Corn chowder

   ■ Creamy potato

   ■ Thai rice

   ■ Garden split pea

   ■ Lentil with couscous

   ■ Zesty black bean

■ **Dried fruits and berries.** These are wonderful as snacks straight from the package or as toppings for cereals and desserts. Stewed fruit is reconstituted in water.

■ **Flavored dried cereals.** Very high-quality flavored cereals can be found in most supermarkets. Hot banana nut barley, cranberry orange oatmeal, wheat 'n' berries, or apple-cinnamon oatmeal—what a lazy way to start a day!

## Just Can It!

Canned foods have long had their place in American kitchens. There are two great advantages in using canned foods. First, they allow you to stock significant quantities of fruits and vegetables for considerable periods of time. Secondly, many canned vegetables and fruits come peeled, boiled, skinned, sliced, diced, or pureed. Additionally, many canned fruits and vegetables are happily married by the canner with spices and other complementary foods. Think about these options:

- **Beans.** Mixed varieties of beans, spiced beans in many flavors, and beans and vegetables are all simple to use and excellent for most dishes. Their advantage over dried beans is that you skip the soaking step. After all, who hasn't forgotten to soak the beans overnight?

- **Tomatoes.** The variety of canned tomatoes, sauces, and pastas runs the gamut of tomato types. What a joy to be able to avoid peeling and chopping or dicing tomatoes. Canned tomatoes are often mixed with onions or pepper for use in Italian- or Mexican-inspired dishes.

- **Pastas sauces.** Next time you hit the grocery store, check out the fresh pasta section and be prepared to be amazed by the variety of prepared sauces waiting for you to take them home! We're no longer bound by whatever Prego decides to put in a jar anymore (although even the oldest jarred tomato sauce maker has expanded exponentially in this area!).

### QUICK ⬛ PAINLESS

To prepare an effortless, healthy, and tasty snack lunch that requires no refrigeration and will not leak or get soggy, throw in a single, prepackaged, ready-to-use dried soup mix and a plastic bag of dried fruits or berries.

■ **Vegetables.** Canned yams and new potatoes come highly recommended because they are already peeled, and that makes me happy. These are my favorite canned products, but if you are saving time by not using fresh vegetables, use frozen vegetables for single-item side dishes.

■ **Fruits and berries.** Like canned vegetables, canned fruits have the advantage of being peeled and sliced, chopped, chunked, or crushed. Canned fruits tend to be less satisfactory for most uses than frozen fruits, but they do make handy side dishes and toppings for desserts. Canned berries are also superior for pies and other desserts.

## FOR SERVICE AND INFORMATION: SPECIALTY AND ETHNIC FOOD STORES AND FOOD CO-OPS

Take advantage of the wealth of specialty food stores that abound. Shed your fears, throw off your hesitation, and plow right into the nearest specialty food store. These small operations can provide you with a world of information and assistance, and in the long run, they will make your cooking life much simpler, more vibrant, varied, and interesting, as well as more successful.

Specialty food store employees, from owners to clerks to stockers, are usually knowledgeable about foods. They will be happy to give you advice about foods, food preparation, and cooking techniques that should save you time. These stores often have an old-fashioned-general-store ambiance.

Buy grains, flour, and other foods in bulk at specialty and ethnic stores. Specialty stores will almost invariably order and stock hard-to-find foods at your request.

Finally, don't underestimate health food stores. See what they have to offer.

## ULTIMATE EASE: SUPERMARKET DELIS AND SALAD BARS

Both delis and salad bars have become a real boon to the easy ways I use my lazy vegetarian kitchen. Even the last-minute vegetarian cook can look like a star by shopping both delis and salad bars. Salad bars often have dozens of items. If you are particularly harried or if you have a need for small batches of vegetables, fruits, greens, and even soups, the salad bar is the perfect solution.

Your supermarket deli and salad bar were designed to make picnic, potluck, and carry-in food preparation time completely unnecessary.

Salads created by supermarket delis are helpful. For picnic and potluck convenience, choose from the deli-made American, German, or mustard potato salad, macaroni salad, three- or four-bean salad, or creamy or sweet-and-sour coleslaw.

Here are some of my favorite vegetarian salads from my local deli counter:

- Artichoke salad
- Greek rotini salad
- Italian vegetable salad
- Pasta and asparagus salad
- Rocky Mountain potato salad

**A COMPLETE WASTE OF TIME**

The 3 Worst Things to Do When Preparing for a Picnic:

1. Make and bag ice.
2. Decide to make deviled eggs.
3. Make your own potato or pasta salad from scratch.

## HOLDOVERS, NOT LEFTOVERS

I do not bungee-jump, skydive, or hang glide. I also never throw away any usable food. Leftovers are a true help to the lazy cook. When making certain foods, such as rice or beans, make extra quantities that you can bag and refrigerate or freeze. In fact, do not consider leftovers as leftovers: Consider them meals that have been prepared ahead of time. The main idea here is never to have to announce that "We're having leftovers!"

When dining out, don't consider the package that you take home to be leftovers, consider it "carry-out." Never leave restaurant leftovers on your plate—but do put them in your refrigerator and build a meal around them the next evening.

## HEAR YE! HEAR YE! READ ALL ABOUT IT!

Before you jump to Part 3, "On to the Main Event: A Culinary World of Easy, Wholesome Vegetarian Favorite Recipes," where I'll share all sorts of great-tasting vegetarian recipes, there are a few things you should think about.

Even I know how boring it is to read page after page of typed thoughts on vegetarian and healthy ideas. But these are very important pages, so do not skip them. The information on these pages can change the way you cook and think about food. We are so lucky because there are so many time-saving foods and techniques to take advantage of right in our supermarket.

Congratulations! You've maximized your leftovers without resorting to "mystery stew!" Grab a cup of cappuccino at your favorite cafe—you deserve it!

The Lazy Way

The most important things to know are:

- **Garlic comes minced in a jar.** Imagine that—you never have to peel and chop garlic again. You can also get garlic and ginger in combination, a big help when preparing a stir-fry.

- **Chopped onions come frozen.** Always keep them on hand. Use them frozen, no need to defrost—they will heat as you cook. You never need to peel and chop an onion again.

- **Always choose a food already prepared.** For example, you can buy fresh ravioli and spaghetti (at the refrigerator counter) that are ready-made and set to cook.

- **Buy bottled tomato sauces.** The quality is very good, and you can choose from tomato sauce with mushrooms, herbs, and basil. Just heat and serve.

- **Choose interesting pasta.** Pasta comes in so many different sizes and shapes; look them over and choose what is best for you and the family.

- **Buy bottled stir-fry sauce.** It is in the condiment section of most supermarkets. You can avoid making time-involved sauces. It saves about 20 minutes per recipe you use it in.

- **Prepared pesto and red pepper sauce are available.** My sister-in-law just moved, and she told me she had stored away maybe one small case of pesto sauce and dozens of various packaged pastas. She went on to say, "Let it snow, we always have a lazy meal on hand."

**A COMPLETE WASTE OF TIME**

The 3 Worst Things You Can Do When It Comes to Cooking:

1. Assume that to be a "good cook" means you have to do everything from scratch.

2. Spend all your time chopping and dicing when someone else has already done it for you.

3. Assume that a healthy meal must require "slaving over a hot stove."

- **Grated cheese is readily available.** In supermarkets all over the country, grated cheese comes plain or flavored, and some even come with added spices. Some cheeses come lower in fat, which is very nice indeed.

- **Chopped peppers also come frozen.** Can you imagine that you can have minced garlic, chopped onions, and peppers all ready to cook?

- **Check out the frozen vegetables.** They come in so many sizes, sliced, chopped, peeled, and in some cases, roasted and ready to cook.

- **Canned vegetables.** The original lazy vegetables are in cans. Do not overlook canned vegetables.

- **Sun-dried tomatoes come chopped.** Just drain and use.

- **Don't forget legumes.** Beans, lentils, and chick peas come cooked and in a can, ready to drain, heat, and serve.

- **Shop the salad bars.** They are amazing. Buy $1/2$ cup of this and that to top off a casserole or salad. For the most lazy among us, it is a great idea. You can buy cups of this and that already sliced, chopped, and grated.

- **Use neighborhood restaurants as a resource.** See what they will sell for take-out. That is, see who will sell plain pasta or ask the Chinese restaurant for cooked rice. You will be surprised at what is available.

YOU'LL THANK YOURSELF LATER

Love garlic but hate chasing those pesky little cloves around the chopping board with a knife? Don't fret! Someone actually gets paid to cut it for you! All you have to do is find it in the grocery store!

- **Give the produce section of the supermarket another chance.** You will find lettuce, baby spinach, and combinations of tasty lettuces, all prewashed and cut, ready to serve. Beside salad greens, you will find handy packages of grated or peeled and washed baby carrots, sliced red cabbage, and washed, peeled whole, quartered, or sliced potatoes of various types. Broccoli comes grated, too, a good idea to add to most salads.

- **Check out the dessert selections.** Somehow I always gravitate to dessert. Look again at the cake-mix section of the market. They have come into a new age! Try muffins—just add eggs and a liquid. Cakes, brownies, lemon squares, and more are enriched and easy to prepare, and they have a long shelf life. Many teens like to bake these cakes. Encourage your children to bake. Of course don't overlook flavored yogurt, ice cream, or fresh fruit. Fresh fruit and perhaps a slice of appropriate cheese is still a wonderful dessert.

- **Puff pastry comes ready-made.** So do pie crusts, cookie dough, and cookie crumbs.

**IF YOU'RE SO INCLINED**

Picture this: It's 4 pm and you've just remembered that you had promised to make dinner for your boss and a few of your coworkers. Don't panic! Pick up the phone and call the nearest restaurant that delivers. They might have just what the doctor ordered!

## Getting Time on Your Side

|  | The Old Way | The Lazy Way |
|---|---|---|
| Chopping vegetables for a salad | 1 hour | Done! |
| Figuring out meal portions | Um . . . still thinking | Don't have to! |
| Washing vegetables | 15 minutes | Don't have to (if you buy prepackaged!) |
| Making fresh pasta | Hours | No need! |
| Making pasta sauces | All afternoon | It's ready! |
| Chopping garlic | 15 minutes | It came that way! |

# Chapter four

# Using Shortcuts and Creativity to Make Your Vegetarian Cooking Life Simple, Simper, Simplest

**O**ver the years I have boiled down my cooking process to a series of steps, which I try to follow carefully and consistently. When that happens, vegetarian cooking is a simple pleasure rather than a chore.

## DIVIDE AND CONQUER

To avoid having your cooking duties control your life by becoming a ceaseless jumble of up-and-down, back-and-forth efforts, break up the entire process into a series of steps.

- Planning
- Shopping
- Storage

- Setup
- Food preparation
- Cooking
- Presentation

At first view this may appear to make cooking a complicated process, but, in fact, one step prepares you for and overlaps with the next step so that the cooking process becomes similar to working a large, simple, seven-piece child's puzzle.

## Planning: Try Something New

Planning meals is a lot like getting organized in life. We expend so much energy in avoiding the process that we never get to it. It's a vicious cycle: more wheels spinning, more time wasted, and more organization to attend to. However, planning your meals on a weekly basis will simplify your life more than any other single effort. Here are some reasons people use to resist meal planning:

- **Not enough time.** You probably don't have the time because you are so busy running off to the grocery or scouring your cabinets for last-minute meals, which must then be prepared and cooked from the ground up.

- **Too many family food preferences and varied schedules.** Meal planning will force a good deal of structure on these variances. You will also prepare yourself to handle food eccentricities and last-minute schedule changes with far greater aplomb.

*QUICK* ☐ *PAINLESS*

Follow this seven-step plan for cooking—plan, shop, store, setup, prepare, cook, and present— and you'll find that cooking healthy meals for your family will truly become "quick 'n' painless!"

- **I don't know how to go about it.** Come on, you do it constantly—one scrambling meal after another.

- **I can never think of what to serve ahead of time.** Well, this isn't exactly like catering your daughter's wedding. Use the recipes in this book to guide you, and browse that dusty library of cookbooks you have built up over the years.

The advantages of meal planning are so manifold that only a few can be listed here.

- **Improved family nutrition.** Last-minute meal preparation not only takes more time, it encourages the worst type of eating habits. Fast-food and "junk" food are so prevalent because so few people plan a week's meals at a time. By planning ahead you will become far more conscious of balancing your family's diet, providing for minimum daily requirements in the various food groups, and in including the necessary vitamins and minerals. Meal planning is also a terrific way to initiate a pattern of more healthful eating.

- **More meal variety.** Variety is the spice of life—and cooking. If your family's nightly anthem seems to be "What, eggplant Parmesan again?" you can break this rut by planning your meals on a weekly basis. Your family will think you've hired a private chef, and so will you.

- **Reduced grocery shopping.** Ever find yourself at the supermarket twice in one day? You could plan a

**A COMPLETE WASTE OF TIME**

The 3 Worst Excuses You Can Give for Not Planning Your Meals:

1. I don't have enough time.

2. I'll never find enough things that everyone likes.

3. I don't know how.

week's meals in the time you expend during that second trip.

- **Less mealtime anxiety.** Too often in American kitchens that last-minute question "What will we have for dinner?" turns into "Where will we go for dinner?" Save stress and scads of money by having an instant, definitive answer to "What's for dinner?"

Here is some advice on meal planning. These are not engraved laws. Adapt these ideas or devise your own system for meal planning. Just do it.

- Choose a definite day of the week and a specific time for meal planning. Limit yourself to 15 minutes (or any given amount of time) for each week's planning. Try your best to stick to this schedule and time limit like burrs on socks.

- Base your weekly grocery shopping lists on that week's meal plans. Compare the ingredients you have on hand with those you need. Add the fresh ingredients that will be necessary for the week's meals, and presto! A shopping list for the entire week.

## Shopping: Once a Week, Not Twice a Day

Try to base all of your supermarket labor on your weekly meal plans. Occasionally you will need to purchase fresh ingredients more than once a week, but don't make it a habit.

- Select one particular day of the week and a particular time of day to do your weekly supermarket shopping—perhaps a weekend midmorning (here's a tip

*QUICK* 🔘 *PAINLESS*

At the beginning of each monthly section in your meal-planning notebook, use a highlighter to mark birthdays, parties, teas, and special events. Make it a habit to consult your monthly planner before planning each week's meals and plan those meals accordingly.

though: Saturday's the worst day of the week) or a weekday after 7 pm. This will ensure the least amount of unwanted company, the most deserted aisles, and the shortest checkout lines.

- Do not allow yourself to become distracted at the supermarket. The only distraction you should entertain should be to consult with the various department managers who have become your confidants and food advisors.

- Organize your shopping list based upon your knowledge of supermarket layout. Move methodically throughout the market. If you must backtrack, make that journey the last one of your shopping trip in order to cut random wandering to an absolute minimum.

- Every week, thoroughly examine your cabinets, pantry, drawers, refrigerator, and freezer, and make a restocking shopping list. Only during this once-a-week shopping trip, take advantage of coupons, supermarket specials, and any desire to try new products. If you use this strategy, you will find that:

  1. You save considerable amounts of money.
  2. Your stocks of staples are always full.
  3. You throw away fewer strange, impulsively purchased foods.

## Storage: Put It Away; Don't Throw It Away

One could probably feed the Chicago Bears well for a day with just the food that had to be thrown out because it

### IF YOU'RE SO
### *INCLINED*

As you start to develop meal planning, use the tried-and-true meal favorites of your family. This way, you will not have to tax your imagination and take extra time to think up new meals. Make the first few weeks of meal planning into a family effort. Soon it may actually become a center of family involvement and cooperation.

was not stored properly. Okay, that may be an exaggeration, but too often fruits and vegetables may look fine but haven't been stored properly and are now questionable. Shall we say it another way? It is essential to store food properly.

- After shopping, immediately store every food product in the proper manner. The whole purpose of storing food properly is to ensure that it retains its freshness and quality.

- Be sure to store the items that you plan to use for the current week's meal in an accessible place. Do not relegate them to pantries. Abiding by proper storage guidelines, store them in the order that you will use them.

- Based upon your weekly meal planning, you should move items that have been placed in long-term storage into a more accessible location. Do this at the same time you store the week's supermarket purchases.

## Setup: Get Ready and Set Before You Go

I mean, really, when I search for an hour throughout my house, tear out some hair, then find my reading glasses on top of my head, I realize why it is so incredibly easy to forget to do so many things to be absolutely ready to cook a meal.

- If you forget to thaw a necessary item, move to the next meal on your week's meal plan and push that day's meal back one day.

YOU'LL THANK YOURSELF LATER

**Learn to read nutrition labels on all prepackaged foods. Check out serving sizes, fat content, and cholesterol. Look for good sources of fiber and check the sugar content. Look at amounts of calcium and vitamin C in the product. You will find that you can quickly distinguish the real quality (or lack of it) in various foods.**

If you take a little time to set up and arrange the foods, spices, and cooking utensils that you will use in the preparation of any meal, you will save time, energy, stress, and both personal danger and burned foods. Unless you have the requisite cooking utensils and vessels stored on easily accessible hangers near the work area, you will need to get them set up to facilitate the cooking process. For instance, place pots and pans on burners and place the following items, in order of use, near your cutting board, work surface, and stove:

- All food products that must not be refrigerated.
- Move refrigerated products you will use to the front and center of the refrigerator.
- All spices and herbs in the order that you will use them.
- All mixing bowls, measuring cups and spoons, spatulas, stirring spoons, and other utensils.
- The food processor, blender, wok, and other kitchen appliances you will use.
- Plenty of pot holders (you will save so many kitchen towels).

Once you arrange all of the materials that will be required to prepare the meal at hand, you will find that your kitchen looks much like that of a famous chef on television. If you have ever marveled at the facility and simplicity with which TV cooks seem to be able to "throw together" the most complicated gourmet meals, well,

## IF YOU'RE SO
# *INCLINED*

Use either self-adhesive labels or colored dots to indicate date of purchase and date of maximum storage on each food product that you bring home and store for later use. This can be the simplest and most effective time-saver in the long run. Before you sit down to make your weekly meal plans, check the labels or colored dots to see what items have reached the end of their shelf life and should be used during that week.

now you know their secret! Proper setup is the secret key to that apparent ease.

## Food Preparation: Doing the Dirty Work

Food preparation is the only really work-oriented process in putting together a meal. Cooking takes its share of time and a bit of effort, but food preparation always takes more.

- Wash and dry all food items at the same time. Do not move back and forth between your work area to wash each item separately. Dry the foods together, using paper towels, rack areas, or spinners.

- Use your appliances to your greatest convenience. If you use your food processor, prepare all foods in the following order to avoid having to clean the processor between each use:

    1. Dry foods first. If necessary, wipe out the processor with a paper towel after each dry food has been processed.

    2. Solid fruits and vegetables with water content, cheeses, and tofu. Slice and dice fruits and vegetables first, starting with the blandest—celery, zucchini, potatoes—and working to the strongest—onions, radishes, and garlic. You will not need to clean the bowl between items until you have processed the strongest foods. If you shred foods, you will probably need to wipe the bowl with a wet paper towel after processing each item. Depending on the liquid quantity, odor, and residue strength of the

processing, you may have to wash the bowl thoroughly with soap and water.

3. Wet foods last. It will be necessary to wash out the bowl between processing of sauces, purees, and marinades.

YOU'LL THANK YOURSELF LATER

Date each week's meal plan and save it. It's easy to rotate or repeat an entire week's meals in alternate months. Devise a simple code or color system to mark each meal as a family hit, miss, or so-so.

■ If you use your chopping block for peeling or mixing foods, wipe the board with a damp paper towel between jobs. (I hope that you are not hand chopping, slicing, dicing, or shredding anything but the most minor items that are so simple to deal with that they defy taking the time to set up, use, and clean the food processor.)

■ Use both fruits and vegetables with the skin on whenever possible to save time and effort and to retain the greatest amounts of fiber, vitamins, and minerals. If you need to peel soft fruits, drop them into boiling water for about 45 seconds, then rinse them under cold running water. The skin will split and lift right off.

■ To avoid the discoloration of freshly cut fruit, submerge it in water to which you have added the juice from half a lemon.

■ If you are going to cook pasta and have a choice as to the pasta type, remember that thin pasta cooks quickly. Angel-hair pasta, for instance, cooks in just three to four minutes. Couscous is even quicker.

■ There are as many food preparation shortcuts as there are cooks with imagination. Try these simple ideas:

Store your most fre-
quently used kitchen
utensils, pots, pans, and
accessories in areas that
are already convenient to
cooking, and you won't
have to move them again
later when you need
them.

■ Avoid hassling with chopping fresh onions in a recipe and substitute frozen onions.

■ To save time when baking potatoes, use bak-ing nails or slice the potatoes in half length-wise and bake cut face down on a greased or sprayed nonstick cookie sheet.

■ Steam two or more vegetables simultaneously in your steamer. Wrap them loosely in alu-minum foil to preserve separate flavors.

■ Place soft cheeses in the freezer for a few min-utes to make them easier to grate.

■ If your kitchen wastebasket is not usually kept close to your work area, move it. Do not walk back and forth to a wastebasket at the other end of the kitchen.

■ If your kitchen space allows, set serving bowls and individual dinner plates on counter space between the stove and the dining area.

## Your Stove (or Grill) Is the Real Cook in the Family

If you have taken advantage of the food preparation step, the cooking process itself should be simple. You should have one or two pleasant alternatives: Either you have a meal based on quickly cooked dishes, in which case you will be eating in very short order, or you have a nice, relaxing break while the food cooks.

Timing is everything. Before you turn the heat on any dial, first make a quick coordination plan. You don't need to write this down, just be aware of cooking times for your various dishes. Consider cooling times and time for the movement of hot foods from the cooking surfaces to the table. Much of the stress that occurs in the kitchen is a result of hit-and-miss procedures. Don't let the boiling water, the bubbling sauces, the steaming vegetables, or the baking goods control and rule your life. Remember, it's your kitchen, and you're in charge!

Make your cooking process into an assembly line. Do not try to rinse pasta with one hand while buttering rolls with the other. Complete each cooking follow-up task before you begin the next one. If you have a cooling time plan in mind and have decided on an order of operations, this should prevent much of the frustration traditionally created by the dreaded "bring it all together" step.

If dessert is on the menu, take a moment while your main courses are cooking to complete any necessary chores that the dessert will require. This is particularly important if it is inconvenient and destructive to family harmony for you to leave the table and put the finishing touches on desserts while the remaining diners wait at the table.

Consider the kitchen to be sacred ground during the cooking process. The old saying, "too many cooks spoil the broth," has not become a truism for nothing. Although it can be advantageous to allow and encourage cooking to be a mutual family effort, make sure you can eliminate confusion by assigning everyone his or her own space and assignment. I appreciate the fact that everyone is driven by human nature to wander into the

Congratulations! You cut the preparation time for your family's favorite casserole in half, and now all you have to do is wait while the oven does its job. Why not get everyone involved in a game while you wait?

kitchen during the cooking; however, unless you have a kitchen like that of Louis XIV at Versailles, you must discourage demands on your space, your time, and your attention.

Finally, ladle cooked foods directly from the pans into serving bowls. While family members and guests seat themselves, place plates and serving bowls on the table. After that, it's every man for himself! By doing it this way, your guests will be sure to get exactly what they want, and in the amounts they desire!

## Presentation: Form and Function

As a coup de grace, elevate every meal to the level of an event. Decorate the table with flowers or a seasonal centerpiece and serve attractive dishes. It takes almost no time to add a parsley sprig or small garden bloom to the corner of a plate. The effect is psychologically positive. Instead of merely feeding, we are dining.

# Getting Time on Your Side

|  | The Old Way | The Lazy Way |
|---|---|---|
| Running to the store | 2 times a day | Once a week |
| Time spent at the supermarket | Hours | 45 minutes |
| Figuring out "what's for dinner" | 15 agonizing minutes a day | 45 minutes a week |
| Preparing the meal | 1 hour | 30 minutes (tops!) |
| Cooking the meal | 2 hours | Half the time |
| Enjoying the meal | Who has the energy? | Pure bliss! |

# Clean Up, Don't Move Out

**W**ho hasn't stood in utter dismay facing a kitchen that looked as though it were facing the after effects of a Roman orgy? How could two hours of meal preparation, gobbled down in 15 minutes by hungry family or friends, produce hours and hours of kitchen cleanup?

The problem is "how" to clean up. Generations of parents and grandparents have dedicatedly instructed their progeny in how to cook, lovingly handing down the treasured family recipes and cooking secrets. What is neglected is cleanup training. So, now some training; take it to heart and the cleanup chore will seem to disappear.

## CREATE AND LIVE BY A WHOLE NEW CLEANUP PARADIGM

Cleaning up your kitchen is not an after-the-meal job. Cleanup should be an ongoing process, and you should have very little cleanup work remaining after you serve the meal. By all

**A COMPLETE WASTE OF TIME**

The 3 Worst Things You Can Do When It Comes to Cleaning Up:

1. Put it off until later.

2. Assume the "elves" will take care of it while you're not looking.

3. Don't clean as you go.

means, make cleanup an integral part of the planning, the food preparation, and the cooking steps.

Before you begin food preparation or cooking, think about the absolute minimum number of pots, baking dishes, and tableware you will need. If you follow some of these guidelines, you'll be on the fast track to the lazy cleanup in no time!

- Plan to use the same pot for multiple uses if you can. Plan to steam foods together in one steamer. Too often kitchen cooks use more equipment than is necessary.

- Be sure that your dishwasher is not already full of clean (or dirty) dishes and that your kitchen wastebasket is empty.

## DURING THE COOKING STAGE

The trick to cleaning as you go is to set yourself up with a routine. Once you start, you'll find it hard to stop!

Put away each single-use item immediately after you use it. This includes all spices, condiments, margarine, milk, cooking sprays, pasta and rice containers, bread bags, and cooking oils. As a reminder, leave the cabinet door open. Use the item, and then put it away automatically.

Keep a plastic or rubber dish drainer near your sink when you prepare food or cook. Many kitchen utensils and devices, such as strainers, colanders, salad spinners, stirrers, measuring cups, knives, and holding plates, often do not need to be washed thoroughly in soapy water. They need to be rinsed in hot water immediately after use and placed directly into the dish drainer to dry. During your final kitchen cleanup, these items should be dry and ready to put away.

■ Use aluminum foil liberally. You can line baking sheets, and all you need to do to clean them afterward is throw away the foil.

■ Use a large soup pot or kettle to simultaneously boil several sealed plastic bags of leftovers or prepared foods. If the food is securely sealed, you should never have to scrub the pot. Immediately after use, rinse it and put it in the dish drainer. Before you try this though, make sure the bags you're using are approved for boiling.

■ For easy cleanup, use liberal sprayings of cooking oil on the surfaces of all cooking containers to which food is likely to stick, such as pasta dishes and pots, the blade of your food processor, casserole dishes, and pizza, cake, pie, and cookie pans.

■ Wipe all food preparation and cooking surfaces regularly with damp paper towels. This will prevent food from hardening and sticking. After each use, throw the towel away. You won't have to wash out your sponge or wiping cloth.

■ After using your oven, wipe the surfaces and racks while it is still warm rather than allowing it to cool completely. If you make this a regular practice, you will save hours of dirty, greasy, arduous labor since food and spill-overs will not have the opportunity to become a fossilized mass that you will then have to remove with a chisel or a cutting torch.

## QUICK ⬤ PAINLESS

If you need extra space to facilitate simultaneous cleanup and cooking, particularly when you are cooking for larger-than-normal numbers, place serving trays or cookie sheets across open drawers. Be sure not to cover drawers that you will need to use during preparation or cooking.

■ Many vegetable scraps do not grind up well in a garbage disposal. To avoid facing the unpleasantness, not to mention the time, of taking a plunger to a clogged sink, toss carrot peels, celery scraps, and all other stringy vegetable parts and peels into your kitchen wastebasket as soon as they accumulate.

## DISH WASHING

The kitchen cook should never be the kitchen slave. It is imperative that each member of the family does his or her share in the cleanup department. The most sensible and easiest task is to take plate, glass, and silver to the kitchen, rinse, and place in the dishwasher. If each member also takes one serving bowl or other item from the table to the dishwasher, no one will be overworked.

After the meal, move all other dishes from the now cool, soapy water and place them directly into the dishwasher. Don't waste time rinsing each item unless it definitely needs further attention. Most people actually wash their dishes twice, once by hand and then once again by dishwater. Save your energy and let the dishwasher do the pot scrubbing.

If you do not have a dishwasher, I would strongly consider putting one on your Christmas list. However, if you must do the dishes by hand and you have a double sink, fill one with hot, soapy water, the other with hot rinse water. If you have only one kitchen sink, fill it with hot, soapy water and use a large, plastic tub as the rinse sink. Start with the cleanest pieces, probably the rinsed

YOU'LL THANK YOURSELF LATER

Use as few platters and serving bowls as possible. Let a large platter hold several foods and even combine foods using separate sides of a bowl. Or better yet, purchase a couple of divided bowls to use during your meals.

dinner plates, then the drinking glasses and cups, next the silver, and finish with any cooking containers.

You may want to wash fine china and crystal by hand. If you do, place a teaspoon of vinegar in the dishwater. This should prevent watermarks while drying in your dish drainer.

If you have cleaned most of your utensils and pans as you used them, dish washing should be a quick and simple task. Under most conditions, even if you have a large family or have entertained guests, it should not take a long time.

Never towel-dry dishes or pans. Use your dish drainer. If you run out of space in the drainer, put a cloth towel on the counter and use it for drying the larger pieces of kitchenware.

## GENERAL KITCHEN PATROL

Periodically, you must give your entire kitchen a cleaning. Give the kitchen a light cleaning weekly, a thorough cleaning monthly, and a nuclear cleaning yearly. The annual cleanup can include behind the stove and refrigerator, the cabinet tops, and those other hideous areas that are usually only thought of when one moves to another apartment or house.

If you clean the kitchen fairly regularly, each cleanup will be much simpler and quicker than if you put off cleaning for long periods of time. Your kitchen will also be much more appealing, healthier, and less likely to harbor bugs and wildlife.

## QUICK ● PAINLESS

Whenever convenient, make a meal into a picnic and serve it on the porch, patio, or deck, using paper plates and cups and plastic silverware. Your family will enjoy the alfresco dining, and the cleanup is simple.

Most people who do not live in a tree house know all about the basic cleaning techniques, such as scrubbing the floor and wiping down cabinets. In fact, you probably have developed your own time-saving ideas and shortcuts. Here, however, are some general reminders and hints that may be helpful:

- First, and most basically, work from the ceiling down! Going the other way will just mean you'll end up sweeping five times instead of once!

- Thoroughly wash your cutting board after you use it. Bacteria prosper in the nicks and crevices of the board. Deodorize the board occasionally by scrubbing it with $\frac{1}{2}$ cup of baking soda dissolved in a quart of warm water. Rinse it and allow it to dry.

- Clean out your refrigerator every garbage pickup day. That way you will prevent unpleasant odors, spoiled foods, and excess clutter. Deodorize the refrigerator by keeping an open box of baking soda or a bowl of charcoal briquettes on a shelf at the rear.

- Wipe the front of your refrigerator and stove frequently. If you don't, you will soon become immune to the sight of the grime, and the only people to notice it will be your guests.

- Clean all of your kitchen appliances, large and small, regularly. There are many toasters that appear to have been blowtorched. Baking soda dissolved in warm water will remove many burn and usage stains from appliances.

## QUICK 🔲 PAINLESS

Cover the top of your refrigerator with a towel or a sheet of waxed paper. Since you probably rarely clean the top portion, when you do think of it, you can simply throw the towel in the laundry room or throw away the waxed paper.

- Run a pot of pure (white) vinegar through your coffee maker at least once a month to clean it and remove coffee stains. Be sure to rinse thoroughly!

- Clean your stove burner liners regularly. Occasionally run your ice-cube trays through the dishwasher—top rack only.

- Send your pot holders through the gentle cycle of your washing machine every now and then.

- If your freezer is not self-defrosting, defrost it when the frost is no greater than $1/2$ inch thick. If you don't, you will increasingly lose freezer efficiency. After you have defrosted, spray the walls of the freezer with cooking spray. Frost will not build up as quickly, and the next time you need to defrost, the ice will slide right off with a slight pressure.

YOU'LL THANK YOURSELF LATER

If you have kitchen cabinets that are not flush with the ceiling, cover the tops with newspaper or aluminum foil. During your semi-annual cleanup, it is off with the old and on with the new. Line your food cabinets with a washable self-adhesive liner, or, even easier, some washable latex kitchen paint (it won't curl up on you!).

## Getting Time on Your Side

|  | The Old Way | The Lazy Way |
|---|---|---|
| Cleaning up after cooking | Hours | 30 minutes (tops!) |
| Scraping dried food off your pots and pans | Hours | No need! |
| Chiseling dried food off the stove | Hours | No need! |
| Cleaning the top of the fridge | A very scary 30 minutes | 2 seconds |
| Cleaning out the inside of the fridge | I'm too scared of what might be in there to even look! | A few minutes each week |
| Defrosting the freezer | All day | 30 minutes |

## Part 3

# On to the Main Event: A Culinary World of Easy, Wholesome Vegetarian Favorite Recipes

## Are You Too Lazy to Read On to the Main Event: A Culinary World of Easy, Wholesome Vegetarian Favorite Recipes?

**1** The thought of vegetarian food makes you think of tasteless piles of raw vegetables. ☐ yes ☐ no

**2** The last time you had a vegetarian meal was, oh, never. ☐ yes ☐ no

**3** You still feel like a little kid at the dinner table when someone tells you to "eat your vegetables!" ☐ yes ☐ no

# Chapter six

# Pop It, Don't Drop It! – Appetizers and Pizza

**M**ark Twain said, "The only way to keep your health is to eat what you don't want, drink what you don't like, and do what you'd druther not." Does living a good, healthy life really boil down, as most people suspect and fear, to giving up every bad habit? Nope. I stand before you as an appetizer and pizza advocate.

These recipes will provide you with a totally new perspective on both appetizers and pizza. If you watch closely, you will spot both family members and guests hoarding away extra supplies or watching diminishing serving trays with sincere concern. And while they are devouring these culinary treasures as if the world were to end tomorrow, they'll never guess that they aren't getting their full blast of wonderfully disguised junk food.

- Bruschetta
- Warm Brie with Apricots
- Herbed Polenta Wedges

- Spinach Potato Balls
- Almost-Instant Goat-Cheese Spread
- Chick-Pea and White Bean Dip
- Lazy Tapenade
- Goat-Cheese and Garlic Pizza
- Nacho Pizza
- Whole-Wheat Pita Pesto Pizza

## QUICK ⬤ PAINLESS

Why not get your kids on the fast track to eating healthy by making these great treats for them when they are clamoring for something to eat? The great thing about appetizers and pizzas is that they're already "kid-sized!"

# Bruschetta

*Bruschetta is simply a piece of "toast" with little pieces of food arranged on top. Let's make this recipe the toast of the town by choosing your favorite firm, crusty bread and toppings that are readily available and lazy to assemble.*

## Makes 4 to 6 servings

One 10-inch baguette French or Italian bread or crusty, firm bread of choice

$^1/_4$ cup olive oil

1 cup salsa

1   Preheat the oven to 425°F.

2   Cut the bread in $^3/_4$-inch slices.

3   Brush each slice of bread lightly with olive oil using a pastry brush.

4   Put bread slices on a nonstick baking sheet.

5   Bake for a few minutes until the bread is light brown; turn once.

6   Set the toasted bread on a serving platter.

7   Sprinkle the toasted bread with salsa and serve warm.

**IF YOU'RE SO**
## *INCLINED*

Why not let your guests make their own bruschetta? Set out a few bowls of toppings, such as sliced tomatoes, olives, chopped onions, grated cheese, minced garlic, chopped cilantro, snipped fresh basil, and toasted bread. Allow guests to top the warm bread and help themselves.

# Warm Brie with Apricots

*You can substitute sprinkled herbs, sautéed onions, or mushrooms on the brie for a savory change. This is a good lazy recipe for a large crowd. It goes a long way, and it makes a handsome presentation.*

## Makes 8 to 12 servings

One 1-pound round of brie cheese
1 cup apricot jam or 1$^1$/$_2$ cups sautéed onions
Crackers, thin slices of French bread, or apple slices

1 Use a potato peeler or a small sharp knife and peel around the hard outer ridge/rim of the cheese, removing as much of the crust as you can.

2 Line a baking sheet with aluminum foil and set the cheese in the center.

3 Spread the jam or onions over the top of the brie. This much can be done ahead of time. Cover the brie and refrigerate until serving time.

4 When ready to serve, preheat the oven to 350°F.

5 Set the cheese in the center of the oven and bake for 10 to 12 minutes or until the cheese is soft.

6 Remove the cheese from the oven, and using two spatulas, set it on a serving plate.

7 Surround the brie with crackers, sliced bread, or apple slices.

8 Serve the brie immediately.

# Herbed Polenta Wedges

*Polenta is a relatively easy cornmeal dish made with either white or yellow cornmeal that is simmered in water and then cooled and sliced. But you can buy polenta already prepared in the dairy case in large supermarkets.*

*Use chopped sun-dried tomatoes or leftover bits of chopped mushrooms or even wedges of pan-fried portobello mushrooms to change the topping on the polenta.*

## Makes 6 servings

One 24-ounce polenta roll

2 to 3 tablespoons canola blend oil or olive oil

1 tablespoon dried basil

1 tablespoon dried tarragon

$1/4$ tablespoon paprika

1   Discard polenta wrapping and slice it into $1/2$-inch pieces.

2   In a nonstick frying pan, heat the oil over medium-high heat.

3   Fry the polenta slices for three to four minutes on each side until golden brown and heated through.

4   Remove polenta to a serving plate and cut each slice into quarters.

5   In a small bowl, mix together the basil, tarragon, and paprika.

6   Sprinkle the herbs over the warm polenta and serve.

### YOU'LL THANK YOURSELF LATER

If you buy premade polenta, all you'll have to do is unwrap the polenta roll, slice, and either pan-fry or grill it, depending on the rest of the meal. It is perfect for last-minute company!

# Spinach Potato Balls

*This recipe is a natural when you have leftover mashed potatoes or use a mashed potato mix. But don't be squeamish about squeezing out the excess liquid from the spinach! Just grab a few sheets of paper towels to wrap the spinach in, give a few squeezes, and you're ready to go!*

*Serve with Greek olives and diced feta cheese.*

## Makes 6 to 8 servings

One 10-ounce package defrosted chopped spinach

3 cups cooked mashed potatoes

2 eggs

$^1/_2$ teaspoon garlic powder

$^1/_2$ teaspoon dried marjoram

$^1/_2$ teaspoon nutmeg

2 tablespoons olive oil or canola oil blend

1 box toothpicks

1 Squeeze spinach dry using paper towels and place in deep mixing bowl.

2 Mix in mashed potatoes, eggs, garlic powder, marjoram, and nutmeg.

3 Using wet hands, shape mixture into $1^1/_2$-inch balls; place on a tray or plate.

4 In a nonstick frying pan, heat oil over medium-high heat.

5 Fry the spinach balls until cooked crisp and golden brown, turning as necessary.

6 Remove to a serving plate and serve hot. Provide toothpicks.

## QUICK ⬤ PAINLESS

Time to drain the spinach? Don't worry! Just use two or three sheets of paper towels to wrap up your defrosted spinach and give a few strong squeezes.

# Almost-Instant Goat-Cheese Spread

*If you use peanuts in this recipe, make sure to ask your guests if anyone has a nut allergy. Serve with crackers or cut vegetables.*

## Makes 6 to 8 servings

8 ounces plain goat cheese

$1/4$ cup light sour cream or plain nonfat yogurt

3 ounces oil packed chopped sun-dried tomatoes

$1/2$ cup chopped peanuts or currants

Crackers or French or Italian bread to accompany on the side

1 In a medium bowl, crumble the goat cheese.

2 In the same bowl, beat in the sour cream, tomatoes, and peanuts.

3 Serve the spread in a bowl surrounded with crackers or thin slices of Italian or French bread.

YOU'LL THANK YOURSELF LATER

Just have recipe ingredients on hand and when company drops by, whip up this spread up in a flash. You can add chopped green onions and sunflower seeds.

# Chick-Pea and White Bean Dip

*For the very lazy cook, serve this dip with crackers or sliced grain or rye bread. Remember to use previously minced garlic.*

**Makes 6 to 8 servings**

Two 16-ounce cans canellini beans, drained
One 16-ounce can chick peas, drained
4 cloves garlic
3 tablespoons orange juice
1/2 cup fresh basil leaves
Salt and pepper, to taste
Crackers or grain bread to accompany

1 Using a food processor, blend the canellini beans, chick peas, and garlic.

2 Add the orange juice, washed and dried basil leaves, salt, and pepper. Puree until smooth. Taste to adjust the seasonings.

3 Spoon the dip into a bowl, and serve at room temperature with sliced grain bread or crackers.

YOU'LL THANK YOURSELF LATER

**The magic word here is "try." Don't be afraid to try new approaches and combinations—you may discover that you have better culinary instincts than you thought!**

# Lazy Tapenade

*Serve with vegetables and thin slices of French bread.*

## Makes 4 servings

$1/2$ cup pitted black Greek olives

1 tablespoon capers

$1 1/2$ teaspoons Dijon mustard

2 tablespoons lemon juice

$1/4$ cup olive oil

1 Use a food processor or blender and puree the olives, capers, mustard, and lemon juice.

2 With the machine running and in a slow steady stream, add the oil through the feed tube.

3 Continue processing a few seconds longer until the oil is incorporated and the ingredients are smooth.

4 Spoon the tapenade into a serving dish, cover, and refrigerate until ready to serve.

Congratulations! You made this tapenade on Monday, but chilled it until you needed it on Friday! Treat yourself and your guests to some fresh flowers for the house!

The Lazy Way

# Goat-Cheese and Garlic Pizza

*This is a great-tasting pizza and also a great project to get the kids involved in. You can make this with either a premade pizza crust, or you can make your crust from scratch—when you use your food processor to make the dough it's quick and easy! We've included a recipe for a homemade crust that you can make with either whole-wheat flour or cornmeal, but if you really want to do this The Lazy Way, use a ready-made crust at room temperature and you'll be raring to go! Another lazy option is to go with a pizza dough mix—usually all they need is a little warm or hot water and you're on your way!*

**Makes 6 to 8 servings**

## For the crust:

$3/4$ cup whole-wheat flour or cornmeal

2 cups all-purpose flour

$1/2$ teaspoon salt

1 package instant dry yeast

1 scant cup warm water

2 tablespoons olive oil

## For the topping:

3 tablespoons olive oil, divided

6 ounces plain goat cheese

3 cloves garlic

2 red peppers

1   Preheat oven to 425°F.

2   Put the ingredients for the pizza crust into the food processor and run it for 8 to 10 seconds. A dough ball will form.

3   On a lightly floured board, knead the dough for two minutes.

4   Put the dough into a large bowl and cover with a towel. Let it stand for 40 minutes.

5   When you are ready to make your pizza, punch the dough down and roll it out into a circle. There's your crust!

6   Set the crust on a pizza pan or cookie sheet. Brush the crust with half of the oil. As an oil-free alternative, you can also sprinkle cornmeal on the pan first!

7   Crumble the cheese and sprinkle it over the crust.

8   Mince the garlic or put it through a garlic press.

9   Seed and slice the red peppers.

10   Sprinkle the garlic and red peppers decoratively over the pizza.

11   Sprinkle it with the remaining oil.

12   Bake the pizza on the lowest oven rack for 15 minutes or until the crust turns light golden brown.

13   Cut the pizza into slices and serve.

YOU'LL THANK YOURSELF LATER

**If you're ready to get your kids into the act, make sure they get into the cleanup act, too— they're never too young to get started on being efficient with your cooking cleanup!**

# Nacho Pizza

*For appetizers, just cut the pizzas into bite-size pieces and serve.*

## Makes 6 servings

1 loaf bread dough
2 tablespoons olive oil
1 tablespoon cumin seeds
8 ounces ($1/4$ pound) grated Mexican flavored cheese
4 green onions
2 tablespoons canned, prechopped jalapeño chilies

1 Preheat the oven to 425°F.

2 Tear the dough into six equal pieces. Roll out each piece of dough into five- to seven-inch pizza circles. Set them on a nonstick cookie sheet.

3 Brush the pizza circles with oil and sprinkle with cumin seeds.

4 Sprinkle the cheese over the pizza circles.

5 Trim and chop the onions.

6 Drain the jalapeño chilies.

7 Sprinkle the onions and peppers decoratively over the pizza circles.

## QUICK 🐹 PAINLESS

Another way to cut the preparation time for pizza dough is to use defrosted bread dough. Simply bring it to room temperature and roll it out or pat it into a pizza pan or cookie sheet. Brush it with olive oil, and you are ready to top and bake.

8 Bake the pizza circles on the lowest rack for 15 minutes or until the crust is a golden color.

9 Remove the pizza circles from the oven, and set on individual dishes. Serve immediately.

## IF YOU'RE SO
## *INCLINED*

These pizza circles are great for those inevitable hunger pangs! Keep a few in the freezer, all made up, and after a few minutes in the oven you'll have an instant healthy snack, with no cleanup required!

# Whole-Wheat Pita Pesto Pizza

*These pizzas are ideal for a quick lunch, an after-school snack, or even a light dinner. The truly lazy way to do this recipe is to buy premade pita rounds, but once again, we've included the recipe for them just in case you want to get the family into the act! Whether you make them or buy them, this recipe calls for four pita rounds to make eight servings.*

**Makes 8 servings**

## For the pita rounds (yields 12 rounds):

- 1 package active dry yeast
- 1 tablespoon sugar
- 1 cup warm water
- 2 cups bread flour
- $^3/_4$ cup stone-ground whole-wheat flour
- $^3/_4$ teaspoon salt
- 1 tablespoon olive oil

## For the topping:

- $^3/_4$ cup prepared pesto sauce
- 2 cups grated light or regular mozzarella cheese
- 4 tablespoons pine nuts

1 Preheat oven to 500°F.

2 Proof one package active dry yeast with 1 teaspoon sugar and 1 cup warm water.

3 Add the bread flour, stone-ground whole-wheat flour, salt, and olive oil.

## IF YOU'RE SO
## *INCLINED*

It is not difficult to make your own pita bread or have your teenagers make it for you. In our family, each child has a recipe that he or she enjoys making for special occasions.

4 Knead until smooth and let stand covered in a bowl for 30 minutes.

5 Punch the dough down and let it rise for another 35 minutes.

6 Divide dough in 12 pieces and roll them into four- to five-inch rounds.

7 Place the rounds on a nonstick cookie sheet.

8 Cover the rounds lightly with foil and let rise 30 minutes.

9 Bake for five minutes in preheated oven on lowest rack.

10 Preheat oven to 375°F.

11 Open four pita rounds and spread pesto sauce evenly on crusts.

12 Arrange the crusts on a nonstick cookie sheet.

13 Sprinkle cheese and pine nuts over pita crusts.

14 Bake the pizzas in the center of the oven for eight minutes or until the cheese has melted and the crust is hot. Serve immediately.

### A COMPLETE WASTE OF TIME

**The 3 Worst Things You Can Do with Pizza:**

1. Use regular yeast instead of quick-rise yeast.

2. Waste your precious time making home-made pizza sauce.

3. Eat cool pizza instead of piping-hot pizza.

## Getting Time on Your Side

|  | The Old Way | The Lazy Way |
|---|---|---|
| Making a crust | 2½ hours (with yeast) | 0 minutes (with pitas) |
| Putting together your grated cheese | 15 minutes | 2 seconds (buy it that way!) |
| Chopping chilies | 10 minutes | 0 minutes (buy them canned) |
| Making polenta | 20 minutes | 0 minutes (buy it made) |
| Chopping sun-dried tomatoes | 10 minutes | 0 minutes (buy them chopped) |

# Chapter
## seven

# One Meal, Full Deal: Soups and One-Pot Meals

**T**he advantages to cooking a one-pot meal are almost too numerous to count! Not the least of which, of course, is the fact that when you're all done, there's only one pot to wash! These one-pot meals won't leave you wanting more when you're done, as they're full of not only the nutrition you need, but also great-tasting stuff!

What could be more lazy than a recipe that lets you throw all your ingredients into one pot and then walk away until it's done? That's all you have to do here, especially if you've taken my advice and gotten yourself a Crock Pot (the ultimate lazy cooking item!).

So prepare yourself for a new way of thinking! Soup isn't just an appetizer anymore, as the following recipes will prove:

- Barley-Mushroom Soup
- Lazy Vegetable Stock

## QUICK  PAINLESS

Wondering what to put in the kids' bag lunches next week? If you make a double recipe of their favorite soup now, you can have some for dinner and surprise them with their favorite next week—all it takes is a little planning ahead and enough freezer space to keep the soup until you want to use it!

- Tuscan Lentil and Tomato Soup
- Gazpacho
- Barley and Quinoa Soup
- Summer Yogurt Soup with Cucumbers, Tomatoes, and Dill
- Melon Soup
- Cincinnati Chili
- One-Pot Ratatouille in Warm Focaccia or a Hot Dog Bun
- Vegetable Chili

# Barley-Mushroom Soup

*This is a great, filling soup, with lots of mushrooms. Absolutely perfect for a cold winter dinner.*

*Season with three bay leaves if desired, but remember to discard them before serving. You can also add $^1/_2$ cup reconstituted Polish mushrooms to the soup for a deeper, more robust taste.*

## Makes 6 to 8 servings

1 large onion

$1^1/_2$ pounds sliced white mushrooms

2 quarts vegetable stock

1 cup instant pearl barley

One 10-ounce package frozen sliced carrots

1 teaspoon each dried marjoram, dried dill, salt, and pepper

$^1/_2$ teaspoon each pepper and powdered garlic

1 Peel and slice the onion.

2 Spray a large pot—or use 2 tablespoons canola blend oil—and place over medium heat. Sauté the onions and mushrooms until soft, stirring occasionally.

3 Stir in the stock, barley, carrots, bay leaves, and seasonings.

4 Bring the soup to a boil, reduce heat to a simmer, partially cover, and continue cooking for 30 minutes or until the barley and vegetables are tender. Taste the soup to adjust the seasonings.

5 Ladle hot soup into bowls and serve.

**IF YOU'RE SO**
## *INCLINED*

Many soups actually taste better the next day, so since you're already there, why not make enough to freeze or chill for later in the week? It's much easier to double a recipe now and end up with extra than it is to have to do it all over again a few days later!

# Lazy Vegetable Stock

*Stuck with some leftover vegetables? Don't get into the habit of throwing them out—if you save all those bits and pieces in plastic bags and then freeze them, you'll have just what you need next time you want to make vegetable stock!*

*When the stock is done, add salt and pepper to taste. Don't worry about peeling the onions, carrots, and shallots, just make sure you scrub them well. For the ultimate in laziness, here's a tip: Some vegetables—such as carrots and onions—can be bought already scrubbed! Take advantage of all of the frozen and precleaned vegetables that are out there. If, however, you plan to puree the soup vegetables and use them to thicken the stock or as a side dish, it will be necessary to peel them before cooking.*

## Makes 2 quarts stock

$3^1/_2$ quarts water

2 large onions

2 large leeks

4 ribs celery

One 16-ounce package frozen sliced carrots

1 pound celery root or 1 cup fresh parsley

3 bay leaves

$^3/_4$ teaspoon each dried thyme and pepper

Salt to taste

1 Use a large stock pot and add water.

2 Peel and roughly chop onions, wash leeks, celery, celery root, and parsley. Add the vegetables to the pot.

3  Stir in bay leaves, thyme, and pepper.

4  Bring the mixture to a boil over medium-high heat. Reduce
   heat to a simmer. Continue simmering, uncovered for $2^1/_2$
   hours. Occasionally skim off any foam from the top of the
   stock.

5  Cool stock, and discard bay leaves.

6  Season with salt.

7  Strain and reserve stock.

YOU'LL THANK YOURSELF LATER

You will really thank
yourself later if you
make and store home-
made vegetable stock
because it is probably
the most important
ingredient for a good
soup and sauce base. If
you take a little time
now to plan ahead,
you'll be able to get
other things done while
the stock is cooking.

With the addition of any of the following items, you can vary the Tuscan Lentil and Tomato Soup. Try tossing in some cooked rice, noodles, or pasta; then add some croutons, drained chick peas, egg drops, $^1/_2$ cup white wine, or even some whole-wheat tortilla pieces, and you've got yourself a whole new soup!

# Tuscan Lentil and Tomato Soup

## Makes 6 servings

1 large clove garlic

1 large onion

2 tablespoons canola blend oil or olive oil

One 10-ounce package frozen carrots

$^1/_2$ teaspoon powdered garlic

$^1/_2$ teaspoon salt

$^1/_2$ teaspoon pepper

$^1/_3$ cup brown lentils

One 28-ounce can crushed tomatoes, keep the juice

3 cups vegetable stock or tomato juice

1 Peel and mince the garlic.

2 Peel and chop the onion.

3 Heat oil in a large saucepan over medium heat.

4 Sauté the onions and carrots, stirring, until the onions are soft. Sprinkle with garlic powder, salt, and pepper.

5 Blend in lentils, crushed tomatoes, and juice. Simmer soup, partially covered, for 20 minutes, stirring occasionally, until lentils are tender.

6 Ladle the soup into bowls and serve.

# Gazpacho

*If you're looking for a soup that eats like a meal, look no further than your recipe for Gazpacho! This, and your favorite book, is the perfect addition to a nice rainy Saturday!*

## Makes 6 servings

6 large tomatoes

1 large green or red bell pepper

1 large cucumber

1 large onion

$^1/_2$ teaspoon powdered garlic

1 cup vegetable stock or tomato juice

$^1/_2$ cup Italian salad dressing

1 Wash and quarter the tomatoes and pepper. Peel and roughly chop the cucumber and onion.

2 Using a food processor or blender, puree the tomatoes. Add the remaining vegetables and stock. Do this in two batches.

3 Remove the soup to a serving bowl. Mix in the salad dressing. Cover and refrigerate until serving time. Serve chilled.

## A COMPLETE WASTE OF TIME

**The 3 Worst Things You Can Do with Tomatoes for Soup:**

1. Don't buy them canned and peeled.

2. Don't store them properly so they are already over-ripe when you're ready to use them.

3. Don't let them peel themselves—which they will do if you dip them in boiling water first!

# Barley and Quinoa Soup

*Quinoa is an Incan word pronounced* keen-wah. *It is a high-protein, mildly flavored seed. It is available in large supermarkets and in health food stores, and it resembles plump sesame seeds. Usually the quinoa has been prewashed and only requires a quick rinse before cooking.*

## Makes 6 to 8 servings

1 large onion

3 cloves garlic

One 10-ounce package frozen sliced carrots

$^1/_2$ cup regular pearl barley

6 cups vegetables stock

One 16-ounce can stewed tomatoes

1 tablespoon dried oregano

1 cup sliced white or brown mushrooms

$^1/_2$ cup quinoa

Salt and pepper

1 Peel and chop the onion. Mince or pass the garlic through a garlic press.

2 Use a sprayed stock pot or add 2 tablespoons of vegetable oil. Sauté the onion and garlic until tender, stirring occasionally. Add carrots, rinsed barley, stock, tomatoes, oregano, mushrooms, and rinsed quinoa.

## QUICK ☜☞ PAINLESS

This soup adds all the ingredients at one time and cooks them until done. Nothing could be easier! The soup tastes even better after a day or two in the refrigerator.

3 Bring the soup to a boil over medium heat. Reduce heat to simmer and cook, partially covered, about one hour or until all the ingredients are tender. Stir occasionally as the soup cooks.

4 Season soup with salt and pepper.

5 Ladle soup into bowls and serve hot.

Congratulations! You made your stock-pot cleaning effortless by spraying it lightly with oil before you use it! Treat yourself (and a loved one) to a night at the movies!

The Lazy Way

# Summer Yogurt Soup with Cucumbers, Tomatoes, and Dill

*For this soup, there is no need to add liquid since all of the liquid comes from the vegetables. If you choose to cut your own cucumbers, cut them in half lengthwise. With a spoon, scoop out the seeds, starting at the top of the cucumber and pulling down with the spoon. Thinly slice the seeded cucumber. But it is easier (and The Lazy Way) to buy the cucumbers already prepared from the salad bar.*

## Makes 6 to 8 servings

1 large cucumber

2 medium tomatoes

3 cloves garlic

4 cups plain nonfat yogurt, chilled

1 tablespoon dried dill

$^1/_2$ cup chopped walnuts

1 Slice the cucumber in a food processor using the slicing disc. Chop the tomatoes. Mince the garlic or put it through a garlic press.

2 Using a deep bowl, mix the cucumber with the tomatoes and garlic. Stir in the yogurt, dill, and garlic.

3 Ladle the soup into individual bowls. Sprinkle on nuts just before serving. Or you could have the nuts in a bowl and pass them at the table for the guests to help themselves.

# Melon Soup

*Melon is rich in vitamin C and beta-carotene and is often a neglected part of the produce department. Revisit this old friend and see what you've been missing!*

**Makes 4 servings**

1 medium melon, honeydew, or cantaloupe
1 cup orange juice
$1^1/_2$ cups vanilla low-fat yogurt
$^1/_2$ teaspoon ground cinnamon
3 tablespoons candied ginger

1 Peel the melon, discard seeds, and cut in chunks.

2 Process the melon soup in two batches. Puree half of the melon pieces, yogurt, and cinnamon in the food processor. Pour into a bowl. Repeat the procedure and mix the two batches. Taste to adjust seasonings.

3 Chop the candied ginger in the food processor.

4 Ladle soup into individual bowls and sprinkle with ginger.

5 Serve chilled.

## IF YOU'RE SO INCLINED

Is it starting to become impossible to read your favorite recipes through the water spots and food dribbles? Take a little time to type up fresh copies and put them in sheet protectors. Look ma! No spots!

# Cincinnati Chili

*The Cincinnati favorite is a mess of pasta topped with chili, grated cheese, and a sprinkling of chopped onion. Cinnamon is the secret ingredient and sometimes even a few chocolate chips.*

**Makes 4 servings**

1 large onion

2 tablespoons olive oil or canola blend oil

$^1/_2$ teaspoon garlic powder

One 15-ounce can kidney beans, drained

1 cup canned, crushed tomatoes

1 teaspoon ground cinnamon

$^1/_4$ teaspoon ground allspice

$^1/_4$ teaspoon cayenne

$^1/_4$ teaspoon dried thyme

$^1/_4$ teaspoon salt

8 ounces whole-wheat pasta

1 cup (4 ounces) grated part-skin mozzarella cheese

1 Peel and chop the onion.

2 To make the chili first, heat the oil in a large nonstick frying pan that has been sprayed with nonstick cooking spray over medium heat. Sauté the onion, sprinkled with garlic powder, until tender.

3 Add the beans, tomatoes, and spices. Continue cooking, stirring occasionally for about four minutes or until hot. Crush some of the beans with the back of a spoon as the chili cooks.

4 While the chili is cooking, cook the pasta according to package directions.

5 Divide hot pasta among the plates. Ladle chili over the pasta and sprinkle with cheese. Serve hot.

## IF YOU'RE SO
## *INCLINED*

Give your guests the gift of choice: Put out a couple little bowls of different cheeses, Parmesan, mozzarella, cheddar, or Monterey Jack, and see what they go for. They may help you find a new combination that you might not have stumbled upon otherwise!

# One-Pot Ratatouille in Warm Focaccia or a Hot Dog Bun

*Warm corn tortillas can easily substitute for the corn cakes. If you have the time, you can make the ratatouille early in the day and reheat it at serving time. If you'd like a richer flavor, add 2 to 3 tablespoons of tomato paste, garlic powder, and salt and pepper to taste.*

## Makes 6 servings

1 large onion

1 medium eggplant

1 medium-large zucchini

2 green or red bell peppers

$2^1/_2$ tablespoons olive oil or canola blend oil

One 16-ounce can sliced tomatoes, include juice

$^1/_3$ cup Italian salad dressing

Salt and pepper

1 Peel and chop onion and eggplant. Slice zucchini and peppers.

2 Heat the oil in a nonstick frying pan over medium heat. Add the onion and eggplant. Cook, stirring occasionally until the onions are soft.

3 Stir in the zucchini, peppers, tomatoes, and juice. Add salad dressing.

4 Cook covered for 15 minutes. Uncover and cook, stirring occasionally, another 15 to 20 minutes. Salt and pepper.

5 Serve ratatouille hot on two corn cakes per serving or as desired. Try serving the ratatouille hot in warm focaccia or even a hot dog bun or seeded hamburger bun.

## IF YOU'RE SO INCLINED

It's not completely necessary, but if you are so inclined, remove excess liquid from the eggplant by putting the eggplant pieces in a large colander. Toss with 1 teaspoon salt and let stand for 30 minutes. Rinse off the salt and pat the eggplant dry.

# Vegetable Chili

*If you have $^1/_2$ to 1 cup of a cooked grain frozen, this is a good chance to use it. You can add up to 1 cup of cooked brown rice, barley, or couscous to the vegetables.*

**Makes 4 to 6 servings**

1 large onion

2 green bell peppers

One 10-ounce package frozen sliced carrots

One 10-ounce package sliced frozen zucchini

1 tablespoon canola blend oil

$^3/_4$ teaspoon garlic powder

Two 16-ounce cans kidney beans, drained

One 16-ounce can chick peas, drained

One 16-ounce can, sliced tomatoes, including juice

1 teaspoon chili powder

1 teaspoon ground cumin

1 teaspoon salt

1  Chop the onion and peppers. Grate the carrot and slice the zucchini.

2  Heat the oil in a large nonstick frying pan over medium heat. Sauté the onion and garlic until tender, stirring occasionally.

3  Stir in the peppers, carrot, zucchini, beans, chick peas, tomatoes, juice, and spices. Cover and cook for five minutes. Uncover and continue cooking for 10 minutes or until done. Taste to adjust seasonings.

4  Ladle hot chili into bowls and serve.

**QUICK 〰 PAINLESS**

Serve the chili with purchased cornbread. Add your favorite complimentary vegetables as you wish.

# Getting Time on Your Side

|  | The Old Way | The Lazy Way |
|---|---|---|
| Cooking chick peas | 2¹/₂ hours | 0 minutes (buy canned) |
| Chopping onions | 10 minutes | 0 minutes (buy frozen) |
| Chopping and seeding peppers | 10 minutes | 0 minutes (buy frozen) |
| Grating carrots | 10 minutes | 3 minutes (use a food processor) |
| Standing over a soup on the stove | Hours | Not anymore! (you've got a Crock Pot!) |
| Cooking kidney beans | About 2 hours | 0 minutes (buy canned) |

# Chapter eight

# Don't Count the Beans; Savor 'Em: Legumes with Pizzazz

**I**t's so easy to overlook the beans—they're so small, and they never jump out at you and say "Pick me!"—but don't pass them by! These pint-sized goodies are chock-full of nutrients and flavor! They're just too good to pass up!

Whether it's a simple puree or a more complex dish like the Southern Italian-style chick peas, there is sure to be something for everyone! The recipes in this chapter will take you into the amazingly versatile world of the bean:

- White Bean Puree
- Black Beans and Yellow Rice with Island Flavors
- Southern Italian-Style Chick Peas and Tomatoes on Baked Potatoes
- Spinach, Mushrooms, and Kidney Beans
- Pinto Bean Hash
- Refried-Bean Tacos

- Fresh Fennel with White Beans

- French Lentils and Sage

- Yellow (or Green) Split-Pea Pancakes

- Northern Greek Lima Bean Stew

YOU'LL THANK YOURSELF LATER

Remember that lentils can be purchased canned as well as dried. Take advantage of the organically canned lentils and always keep a can on hand.

# White Bean Puree

*Beans are members of the legume family, which also includes split peas, black-eyed peas, kidney beans, navy beans, lentils, soybeans, and chick peas. Beans are rich in fiber with a high carbohydrate content. This is burned quickly by the body and converted into usable energy.*

**Makes 4 servings**

Two 15-ounce cans white beans

2 tablespoons olive oil

$^1/_4$ cup trimmed cilantro

Salt, pepper, and garlic powder to taste

1 Drain the white beans.

2 Using the food processor in two batches, add one can of the beans, the cilantro, and spices. Puree the bean mixture and spoon into a bowl. Repeat the procedure.

3 Serve puree at room temperature. Cover and refrigerate until needed, or if you prefer it hot, heat in a small pan sprayed with nonstick cooking spray. Good as a dip with vegetables or as a dressing over steamed vegetables.

## IF YOU'RE SO INCLINED

When preparing dry beans, I don't feel it's necessary to soak them overnight. Simply rinse the beans and cover with hot water three inches over the beans. Bring to a boil and continue boiling for two minutes. Reduce heat to simmer and cook for two and a half to three hours, until tender. Add water as necessary. Fresh lemon juice is also well worth the small effort to give your beans an extra zing!

# Black Beans and Yellow Rice with Island Flavors

*Rice and beans together create a complete protein. Dried beans are a rich source of protein, calcium phosphorus, and iron. An added bonus: You can store dried beans for up to one year.*

*To cook your rice, follow the package instructions. A general rule of thumb is to use a medium saucepan. Bring the water to boil (2 cups water to 1 cup rice), and add the rice, turmeric, and salt. Cover, and cook over low heat until rice is tender, about 15 to 20 minutes. Cool slightly. This step can be done earlier in the day.*

## Makes 4 servings

2 cups cooked instant white or brown rice

Two 15-ounce cans kidney or black beans

One 16-ounce can tomato slices

$1/4$ red-wine vinegar

3 to 4 drops Tabasco sauce, or to taste

$3/4$ teaspoon ground turmeric

$3/4$ teaspoon ground cumin

$3/4$ teaspoon salt

$1/8$ teaspoon ground allspice

1 Prepare instant rice according to package instructions.

2 In separate bowls, drain the canned tomatoes and canned beans.

YOU'LL THANK YOURSELF LATER

**It is such a good idea to save, package, and freeze $1/2$ and 1 cup portions of leftover cooked rice and beans. For example, this recipe calls for 2 cups of cooked rice. If you happen to have already frozen and stored some cooked rice, you're ahead of the game; just add the turmeric to the rice, and you're good to go!**

3 Using a deep bowl, combine the beans, tomatoes, vinegar, and Tabasco. Add spices. Heat bean mixture in a saucepan over medium heat for three to four minutes.

4 Lightly toss the rice together with the bean mixture.

5 Serve the bean and rice mixture over sliced lettuce or chopped spinach and top with chopped avocado if desired. Good hot or room temperature.

### A COMPLETE WASTE OF TIME

**The 3 Worst Things You Can Do with Beans:**

1. Don't buy them canned.

2. If you buy them dry, forget to precook them.

3. Don't eat them!

# Southern Italian-Style Chick Peas and Tomatoes on Baked Potatoes

*Baking potatoes are grown in many areas of this country, but the most famous are the Idaho and Maine varieties.*

*Chick peas are a dried pea, important in Indian and Mediterranean cooking. They are available reconstituted in cans.*

### Makes 6 servings

6 medium-large baking potatoes

1 large onion

One 16-ounce can chick peas

One 16-ounce can chopped tomatoes

3 tablespoons fresh lemon juice

$1/2$ teaspoon ground cumin

$1/2$ teaspoon garlic powder

$1/2$ teaspoon curry powder

1 Prepare your vegetables in the following manner: scrub the potatoes, drain the chick peas, and drain the tomatoes, but be sure to save the liquid for later use!

2 Preheat the oven to 425°F. Stick each potato, several times, with a knife tip.

3 Bake the potatoes on the center rack of the oven for about one hour or until they test done.

4 While the potatoes are baking, prepare the vegetables. Peel the onion and chop it, or quarter it and process briefly to chop.

## YOU'LL THANK YOURSELF LATER

It is very easy to use fresh lemon juice, but first you should buy a lemon reamer at a cookware store. It takes only one or two turns to have fresh lemon juice. If you can't find a lemon reamer, use prepared lemon juice.

5 Heat a sprayed, nonstick frying pan, or use 2 tablespoons olive oil, over medium heat. Sauté the onion over medium heat until tender. Add the chick peas, tomatoes and tomato liquid, lemon juice, cumin, garlic powder, and curry powder. Continue cooking eight minutes, stirring occasionally. Vegetables should be moist but not dry.

6 Cut potatoes in half horizontally and gently squeeze open. Place potato halves on individual dishes and spoon hot vegetables over top and serve.

## QUICK 🔳 PAINLESS

If you're not sure when your baked potatoes are cooked, here are two ways to check: the potato will test soft when a knife is inserted or when it is squeezed gently.

**IF YOU'RE SO**
**INCLINED**

If you add an additional 1½ cups of cooked, hot kasha or barley to the vegetables before serving, this dish turns into an interesting entree.

# Spinach, Mushrooms, and Kidney Beans

*Between the iron in the spinach, the vitamins in the mushrooms, and the protein in the beans, you can't go wrong with this recipe! Here is one soup that will definitely eat like a meal!*

### Makes 4 servings

1½ cup kidney beans

4 cups presliced white mushrooms

Salt and pepper

6 ounces fresh trimmed and washed spinach (do not drain!)

3 tablespoons Italian dressing

1 Drain the kidney beans.

2 Heat a sprayed nonstick frying pan, or use 2 tablespoons olive oil, over medium heat. Sauté the mushrooms until tender, about five minutes, stirring occasionally.

3 Season the mushrooms with salt and pepper.

4 Trim and wash the spinach, but do not drain. Add spinach. Continue cooking until the spinach has softened but not completely wilted. Splash vegetables with salad dressing and stir to combine. Mix in the beans, heat, and serve.

# Pinto Bean Hash

*The pinto bean is the mottled oval seed of a common shell bean. You can find dried pinto beans in many forms. Whether they are sold in plastic bags, in bulk, or in convenient cans, this is truly a great bean!*

**Makes 4 to 6 servings**

1 large onion
1 large green bell pepper
Two 15-ounce cans pinto beans, drained
One 16-ounce can diced tomatoes, including juice
3 tablespoons vegetable oil
2 tablespoons ground cumin
2 tablespoons chili powder
Salt, garlic powder, and cayenne pepper to taste

1   Peel and chop the onion, and slice the pepper.

2   In separate bowls, prepare your beans and tomatoes by draining them, but make sure to save the tomato liquid!

3   Heat the oil in a nonstick frying pan over medium heat.

4   Sauté the onion and pepper until soft, about four minutes.

5   Add the beans, tomatoes, and spices. Using a masher, gently mash most of the beans as you heat them. Continue cooking a few minutes until heated.

6   Spoon into a bowl and serve hot.

YOU'LL THANK YOURSELF LATER

Just in case you haven't picked up on the subtle hints we've been dropping with each recipe in this chapter: Please use canned beans. It's truly *The Lazy Way* to take advantage of this small, yet powerfully packed protein storehouse! Simply drain, and you're ready to go!

# Refried-Bean Tacos

*This is a great recipe for those ultra-busy weeknights, and one that the kids (and young at heart) are sure to enjoy! To make this an even lazier recipe, prepare the filling in separate serving bowls and let your family and guests build their own dinner!*

## Makes 4 servings

2 cups Pinto Bean Hash (see earlier in this chapter)

$^1/_4$ pound (1 cup) grated Monterey Jack cheese

$^1/_2$ cup plain nonfat yogurt or sour cream

4 plain or whole-wheat flour tortillas

1  Heat a sprayed nonstick frying pan over medium heat. Heat the hash.

2  Spread the hash in the middle of each tortilla. Top with grated cheese and a dollop of yogurt.

3  Roll and enjoy.

# Fresh Fennel with White Beans

These mild-tasting beans combine with the licorice flavor of the fennel to create a bright, fresh dish.

The mild Great Northern bean is a large white shell bean. They are sold canned, in jars, or dried. Do not store them without using them more than one year.

**Makes 4 servings**

1 medium onion

1 large green or red bell pepper

1 large fennel bulb

2 tablespoons olive oil

$^1/_2$ cup vegetable stock

Two 15-ounce cans white beans

Salt, pepper, and dried dill

3 tablespoons balsamic vinegar

1  Peel the onion and chop using a food processor. Slice the pepper. Wash, peel, and slice the fennel.

2  Heat 1 tablespoon of the oil in a sprayed nonstick frying pan over medium heat. Sauté the onion, pepper, and fennel about five minutes, stirring occasionally.

3  Add vegetable stock and continue cooking until the fennel is tender, about five minutes longer.

4  Drain the beans.

5  Stir in the beans and cook until hot. Season with salt, pepper, dill, and vinegar. Add 1 or 2 tablespoons more of olive oil if you are so inclined.

**IF YOU'RE SO INCLINED**

Serve this dish with some hearty French bread on the side for scooping up those last bits in the bowl and you've got a meal to lust for!

# French Lentils and Sage

*Lentils are best when they remain whole, so do not overcook them. They are a disc-shaped seed of a legume plant native to Asia Minor, and their colors range from pink and greenish brown to yellow and orange. Store them in a cool, dry area and remember that you can store them for up to a year before you should restock with a fresh supply.*

**Makes 4 servings**

> 2 cups French lentils
> 1 large onion
> 1 large red bell pepper
> $^1/_4$ cup chopped parsley or cilantro
> 3 tablespoons red-wine vinegar
> Salt, pepper, and dried sage to taste

1 In a saucepan, cover the lentils with about two inches of water. Cook lentils, partially covered for about 20 minutes or until tender, but not mushy. Drain.

2 While lentils are cooking, peel and chop the onion and chop the pepper using a food processor.

3 Put hot lentils in a bowl and toss with peppers, onions, parsley, vinegar, salt, pepper, and sage.

4 Cool to room temperature and serve over shredded lettuce or tomato slices.

**IF YOU'RE SO**
**INCLINED**

Play with your flavoring! You can substitute vegetable stock for the water or even add a couple bay leaves to the lentils as they cook. Just make sure that if you opt for the bay leaves that you discard them before serving.

# Yellow (or Green) Split-Pea Pancakes

*If you're looking for a little variety, try substituting brown rice for the couscous.*

## Make 4 servings

1 cup yellow split peas

1 medium onion

$1/4$ cup seasoned breadcrumbs

$1/4$ cup egg substitute or 1 egg

1 cup cooked instant couscous

Salt, pepper, tarragon, and garlic powder to taste

1 Cook split peas according to package instructions. While the peas are cooking, peel and chop the onion.

2 Using a food processor, combine the cooled peas, bread crumbs, and egg (or egg substitute). Cover and refrigerate for 20 minutes.

3 Stir couscous and spices into the pea mixture.

4 Heat a nonstick frying pan that's been sprayed or use 2 tablespoons vegetable oil. Shape mixture into pancakes, using about $1/4$ cup or the mixture for each pancake. Cook about four minutes or until golden on the bottom. Spray the top of the pancake lightly and turn over. Continue cooking for four minutes until hot and golden.

5 Serve hot. Good with nonfat plain yogurt or chopped tomatoes.

## QUICK ⬤ PAINLESS

You want to be a lazy cook, right? Then make sure that you're food processor does all the work—don't let it languish away, out of sight, while you end up working up a sweat!

# Northern Greek Lima Bean Stew

*Who says a stew has to have meat? Those crafty little beans are coming to the rescue again! Packed with flavor and protein, a good bean stew is not only filling, but also great for those blustery winter nights!*

## Makes 4 to 6 servings

1 large onion

Two 16-ounce cans lima beans

1 cup pre-grated carrots

One 16-ounce can sliced tomatoes, including juice

3 tablespoons tomato paste

$^3/_4$ teaspoon salt

$^3/_4$ teaspoon garlic powder

$^3/_4$ teaspoon dried oregano

$^1/_4$ teaspoon black pepper

1 Preheat oven to 325°F. Use a 3-quart ovenproof casserole dish.

2 Peel and chop the onion in a food processor.

3 Drain the beans.

4 Mix the beans with the onion, carrot, tomato, and tomato paste in a casserole. Season with salt, garlic powder, oregano, and pepper to taste.

5 Bake in the center of the oven for 45 minutes, stirring once during the baking time. Serve hot.

# Getting Time on Your Side

|  | The Old Way | The Lazy Way |
|---|---|---|
| Cooking lima beans | 2 to 2$^1$/$_2$ hours | 0 minutes (buy canned) |
| Using herbs | 10 minutes to trim and chop | 0 minutes (buy dried) |
| Mincing onions | 10 to 15 minutes | 1 minute (use food processor) |
| Getting children to eat beans | 20 minutes | No time, with interesting, tasty dishes |
| Shredding carrots | 15 minutes | 0 minutes (buy them preshredded!) |
| Preparing beans | All night (by soaking) | 2 hours (by precooking) |

# It Just Gets Bigger and Better Every Day: Pasta

**A** wit once remarked, "No man is lonely while eating spaghetti." And I think that pretty well sums up the entire pasta family, which decidedly has more kinks and twists by far. But part of the beauty of pasta is exactly that: It comes in more shapes, sizes, and flavors than you can shake a stick at!

Pasta is very easy to work with and has tremendous flexibility—whether as an entree, a side dish, or a salad (although we don't generally recommend it as a dessert!). The somewhat bland taste of pasta marries well with most herbs and spices, allowing you a wide spectrum in which you can flex your creative powers. Pasta is also complemented in its flexibility by scads of sauces and makes a delicious single-dish lazy meal when tossed with olive oil, butter, margarine, or salad dressing, and of course, tomato sauce. A lazy rule of thumb: Use light sauces for delicate pastas like angel hair and capellini and heavy, thick, and chunky sauces for robust pastas like rigatoni and fusili. Unusual and curious-shaped pastas also are

better suited to lighter sauces so that their quaint and intriguing shapes are not lost in the sauce.

For goodness sake, take advantage of the plethora of fresh pastas now available everywhere. Besides possessing fine quality and fresh taste, fresh pastas cook in a fraction of the time needed for dried pasta. Fresh pasta will keep for several days in the refrigerator and can be frozen for up to a month.

The recipes I'll cover in this chapter are:

- Farfalle Pasta with Black Beans and Tomatoes
- Thai Broccoli over Whole-Wheat Noodles
- Chinese Egg Noodles and Instant Brown Rice
- Stir-Fried Rice Sticks with Vegetables
- Fettuccine with Currants and Pine Nuts
- Penne with Carmelized Onions
- Warm Ravioli Tossed with Hazelnuts
- Whole-Wheat Couscous with Tomatoes and Capers
- Mediterranean Orzo Salad

# Farfalle Pasta with Black Beans and Tomatoes

*Pasta should be just tender, so do not overcook, and always read package directions, as they can vary. Farfalle pasta is bow-tie shape. Substitute firm tofu for the cheese if you wish.*

**Makes 4 to 6 servings**

One 28-ounce can crushed tomatoes, including juice

2 teaspoons dried basil

One 16-ounce can black beans

$^1/_2$ cup sliced black olives

Salt, pepper, and garlic powder to taste

12 ounces farfalle pasta

$^1/_4$ pound (1 cup) sliced sharp Cheddar cheese

1 Heat a sprayed nonstick frying pan, or use 2 tablespoons olive oil, over medium heat. Add tomatoes and basil.

2 Drain the black beans.

3 Reduce heat to simmer and continue cooking for four minutes, stirring occasionally. Stir in the beans, olives, salt, pepper, and garlic to taste.

4 While the sauce is cooking, prepare the pasta according to the package. Drain.

5 In a serving bowl, toss the hot pasta with the sauce and sprinkle with cheese. Serve hot.

**IF YOU'RE SO**
**INCLINED**

Package any leftover black beans in a small self-sealing plastic bag and freeze. They come in handy as a topping, or you can add it to a soup or salad.

If you want to make your own peanut sauce, first mix together 1 tablespoon minced garlic, 1 teaspoon powdered ginger, 3 tablespoons chunky peanut butter, 3 tablespoons light soy sauce, 1 tablespoon sugar, and 2 tablespoons lemon juice.

# Thai Broccoli over Whole-Wheat Noodles

*For a truly lazy approach to this unique recipe, precut broccoli is available at the vegetable counter in supermarkets.*
*For a complete meal add 1 cup firm tofu, diced.*

## Makes 6 servings

1 large onion
12 ounces whole-wheat pasta
One 10-ounce package frozen sliced broccoli
1 cup snow peas
$^1/_2$ cup Asian peanut butter sauce

1 Peel and chop the onion in a food processor. Set aside.

2 Cook the pasta according to the package and drain.

3 Heat a sprayed nonstick frying pan, or use 2 tablespoons vegetable oil, over medium heat.

4 Stir-fry the onion until soft, partially covered. Add the broccoli and stir-fry a few minutes. Stir in the drained noodles and the sauce. Continue cooking just until hot. Serve hot.

# Chinese Egg Noodles and Instant Brown Rice

*Don't forget, pasta doesn't necessarily come only with an Italian name attached! There are some great Asian noodles on the market that you shouldn't overlook!*

*Another variation on this recipe that you can try is to substitute whole-wheat spaghetti for Chinese noodles.*

## Makes 4 servings

$^1/_4$ cup butter or margarine

1 cup thin Chinese egg noodles

2 cups uncooked instant brown rice

4 cups vegetable stock

Salt and pepper to taste

**1** Heat the butter in a nonstick frying pan over medium heat.

**2** Add the uncooked rice and stir to coat.

**3** Add the vegetable stock and reduce heat to simmer, stirring occasionally, until the stock is absorbed and the rice is tender, about 10 minutes. Season with salt and pepper. Cover and let stand for a few minutes before serving.

## QUICK ☜☞ PAINLESS

Steaming is another lazy cooking technique. Fill the steamer or other pot with enough water to come just below the steamer rack. Bring the water to a boil. Reduce the heat to medium. Add vegetables, cover, and steam until done.

# Stir-Fried Rice Sticks with Vegetables

*Try substituting cooked Japanese buckwheat soba noodles for the rice sticks. You can also substitute low-sodium soy sauce for regular soy sauce to keep this recipe heart friendly.*

*Use your food processor to chop and slice vegetables or buy them already prepared in the frozen food section.*

## Makes 4 servings

$1/4$ pound dried rice sticks

$1/2$ cup vegetable stock

$1 1/2$ tablespoons cornstarch

3 tablespoons soy sauce

$1/2$ teaspoon Chinese five-spice powder

$1/2$ teaspoon garlic powder

$1/2$ teaspoon salt

4 green onions

2 green or red bell peppers

1 bok choy

1 Soak the rice sticks in boiling water for 10 minutes or until softened. Rinse and drain. Cut noodles into two-inch lengths with kitchen scissors.

2 Using a small bowl, add the vegetable stock mixed with the cornstarch, soy sauce, and spices. Reserve.

3 Wash and slice the green onions, peppers, and bok choy.

**IF YOU'RE SO**
*INCLINED*

Once in a while, take a trip to an Asian grocery store. Most of the ingredients you'll find there are dried and will last a long time. Be adventurous and try new tastes and spices. Five-spice is a combination of cinnamon, cloves, white pepper, anise, and fennel.

4 Heat a sprayed nonstick frying pan, or use 2 tablespoons of vegetable oil, over medium-high heat. Sauté the green onions, peppers, and bok choy, partially covered, until tender, stir-frying as you cook.

5 Stir in the noodles and the sauce. Continue to stir-fry until heated.

6 Spoon the mixture into a deep bowl and serve.

YOU'LL THANK YOURSELF LATER

Stir-frying saves time and helps to lock in flavor. Just move the food quickly with a spoon or spatula. For the ultimate in lazy cleanup, use a nonstick spatula and pan.

# Fettuccine with Currants and Pine Nuts

*This recipe is so easy, you'll almost forget you spent any time in the kitchen! But don't be deceived—just because it's easy doesn't mean that you're sacrificing the flavor! Currants are a wonderfully tangy berry that make a beautiful marriage with the flavor of the pine nuts.*

*If currants are not available, try raisins. You can also add 1 cup chopped tomatoes, peppers, drained chick peas, or cucumber to the pasta.*

### Makes 4 to 6 servings

12 ounces fettuccine

1 large red onion

2 tablespoons red-wine salad dressing

2 teaspoons ground cumin

2 teaspoons dried basil

$^3/_4$ cup currants

$^3/_4$ cup pine nuts

1 Cook the pasta according to the package and drain. Put it in a serving bowl.

2 Peel and chop the onion. Toss the onion and dressing with the pasta. Mix in the cumin, basil, currants, and pine nuts.

3 Serve hot or at room temperature.

**Congratulations! You whipped up this effortless fettuccine recipe to save the day when your in-laws invited themselves to dinner! I believe your significant other owes you breakfast in bed!**

The Lazy Way

# Penne with Caramelized Onions

*For the very lazy, use a jar of tomato (pasta) sauce and sprinkle with seeds or nuts.*

## Makes 4 to 6 servings

12 ounces whole-wheat penne

3 large onions

$^1/_4$ cup dark brown sugar

$^1/_2$ cup port wine

$^1/_2$ cup pumpkin seeds or chopped hazelnuts

1 Cook the penne according to the package and drain. Set aside.

2 Peel and slice the onions in a food processor.

3 Heat a sprayed nonstick frying pan, or use 2 to 3 tablespoons vegetable oil, over medium-low heat.

4 Add the onions and stir occasionally until golden. Partially cover if they begin to stick. Mix in the sugar and wine. Simmer for four minutes.

5 Put the hot pasta in a bowl and toss with the glazed onions. Sprinkle with pumpkin seeds. Serve hot or at room temperature.

## IF YOU'RE SO INCLINED

Why not make your next dinner party buffet style? Recipes like this Penne with Caramelized Onions are the perfect choice since they don't loose any of their charm when they cool to room temperature!

Ravioli can be made by hand, but for the smart, lazy cook, shop for a good fresh ravioli, located in the dairy case, or use dried. Like pasta, ravioli comes in flavored varieties, from stripped to spinach, and with many flavor fillings, from mushrooms to cheese.

# Warm Ravioli Tossed with Hazelnuts

*Fresh ravioli can be found in the dairy section of the supermarket. If you want you can sauté sliced mushrooms and add them to the sauce. Or pass some grated Pecorino or Parmesan cheese at the table.*

## Makes 4 to 6 servings

Two 9-ounce packages fresh ravioli

One 6-ounce jar pesto sauce

$3/4$ cup chopped hazelnuts

1 Cook ravioli according to the package and drain. Put it in a serving bowl.

2 Toss the hot ravioli with the pesto sauce and sprinkle with nuts.

3 Serve hot or warm.

# Whole-Wheat Couscous with Tomatoes and Capers

*Use either plain or whole-wheat couscous. You can also add 1 cup of white or black beans if you like. Couscous is a relative of the pasta family, and it is the easiest to prepare. Just add it to boiling water, cover, and wait a few minutes until the water is absorbed.*

*For the very lazy cook, toss the cooked couscous with $^1/_2$ cup of salsa. And don't forget: Pistachio nuts come packaged and shelled.*

## Makes 4 servings

$1^1/_4$ cups instant whole-wheat couscous

One 11-ounce can mandarin oranges

$^1/_2$ cup shelled pistachio nuts or chopped pecans

1 Cook couscous according to the package. Fluff the couscous with a fork as you put it in a bowl.

2 Drain the mandarin oranges.

3 Toss the couscous with mandarin oranges and nuts.

4 Serve immediately.

QUICK  PAINLESS

Is someone in the family allergic to nuts? No problem! Just serve the nuts on the side and let everyone serve themselves.

# Mediterranean Orzo Salad

*Orzo, a rice-shaped pasta, is an interesting choice for a change.*

*Add ¹/₂ cup of chopped parsley or cilantro for added color and taste. Season with salt and pepper if desired.*

## Makes 4 servings

2 medium tomatoes

4 cups cooked orzo

¹/₂ cup feta cheese

¹/₃ cup sliced black olives

2 cups rinsed, trimmed, torn spinach

¹/₄ cup red-wine vinegar salad dressing

1   Chop the tomatoes.

2   In a serving bowl, combine the cooled orzo with the tomatoes. Crumble the cheese as you add it to the orzo salad. Toss the olives, spinach, and dressing with orzo.

3   Serve at room temperature.

# Getting Time on Your Side

|  | **The Old Way** | **The Lazy Way** |
|---|---|---|
| Making your own pasta | 1 hour | 0 minutes (buy prepared pasta) |
| Making your own sauces | 30 to 45 minutes | 0 minutes (buy prepared sauces) |
| Chopping vegetables | About 10 minutes | 0 minutes (buy frozen) |
| Using pasta as a side dish | About 30 minutes to make entree | 0 minutes (serve a salad and make pasta an entree) |
| Getting tired of pasta | Often | Never again! |
| Eating boring pasta | All the time | Never again! |

# Don't Discount the Spud, Bud: Potatoes Are Great

**P**otatoes are a treasure trove of essential nutrients. And if you eat the skin, you get the bonus of added fiber. A medium-size baked potato is a nutritional bargain at about 200 calories. It provides almost one-half of your daily requirement for vitamin C, about as much potassium as a banana, almost 5 grams of protein, and a variety of vitamins and minerals. It is cholesterol free and low in sodium. Sweet potatoes also provide beta-carotene, the pigment that gives them their orange color. Beta-carotene is an antioxidant and may help protect against some diseases.

There are eight species and literally thousands of varieties of potatoes. The consumer has about 12 varieties from which to choose. Potatoes are identified by where they were grown (as in Idaho or Maine potatoes), by type (all-purpose, boiling, or new potatoes), or merely by color (white, yellow, red, or blue). When selecting them, look for potatoes that are firm, smooth, well shaped, and heavy. Avoid potatoes that have

YOU'LL THANK YOURSELF LATER

The very lazy might want to use a microwave for baking potatoes. For one potato, pierce the potato in several places and set it on a paper plate. Microwave on high for 8 to 10 minutes per potato, depending on their size. Let the cooked potato stand a few minutes before handling.

sprouted or cracked, that are withered or wrinkled, or that have green or dark discoloration.

When shopping for sweet potatoes, select small or medium specimens, as they are the most tender. To avoid peeling headaches, do not buy sweet potatoes with strange twists or knobs. Generally, the darker the skin, the sweeter and moister it will be.

Put potatoes to use in the recipes in this chapter:

- The Very Best Baked Potato
- Double-Baked Potatoes
- Baked Potatoes with Fajita Vegetables
- Mashed Potato Cakes
- Sweet Potato Wedges
- Steamed New Potatoes
- Zucchini, Carrot, and Potato Pancakes
- Hashed Brown Potatoes
- Sweet Potato Quesadillas

# The Very Best Baked Potato

*Use Idaho or Maine potatoes and choose one that has a thick, crispy skin and is fleshy. Baked potatoes are easy to make correctly. While they are baking, take advantage of the time. Set the table, prepare other dishes, cook something else, or do your nails.*

**Makes 4 servings**

4 well-shaped medium-large baking potatoes

1 Preheat the oven to 425°F.

2 Scrub the potatoes. Stick each potato several times with a fork or the tip of a small, sharp knife.

3 Spray each potato with butter-flavored, nonstick cooking spray—or use oil.

4 Put the potatoes on a cookie sheet and bake in the center of the oven for 45 minutes to one hour, or until the potato tests done. The potato is done when the potato can be pierced easily with a fork.

5 Make a slit lengthwise down the center of the potato. Gently squeeze the sides of the potato until it pops open. Smear with butter and/or plain yogurt.

## QUICK ⬤ PAINLESS

How to tell when a potato is fully cooked? It's easy! Simply grab the nearest (clean) fork and poke the potato in question. If you can pierce it easily, it's ready for dinner!

**IF YOU'RE SO**
*INCLINED*

Make an extra potato or two and cut it up cold for a quick and easy potato salad.

# Double-Baked Potatoes

*Sure, this recipe is simple, but simplicity is key in the lazy kitchen! You'd be surprised how many people are walking around without an idea of how great the potato is for a simple side dish. So, grab a couple spuds and have at it! Consider this your family's new favorite addition to the main course!*

## Makes 4 servings

4 baked potatoes
$^1/_2$ cup plain nonfat yogurt
Salt and pepper
$^1/_4$ cup reduced-fat Monterey Jack cheese

1 Cut baked potatoes in half lengthwise. Scoop out the potato, leaving a $^1/_2$-inch thick shell.

2 Put the potato in a bowl. Mash it using a potato masher. Mix in the yogurt, salt, pepper, and cheese.

3 Put the filling back into each potato shell without packing it down.

4 Set the potatoes on a cookie sheet. Return the potatoes to the 425°F oven and bake for 10 minutes or until hot and crusty.

5 Serve.

# Baked Potatoes with Fajita Vegetables

*Looking for some extra zing with dinner? The lazy solution is to add some vegetables done with a fajita marinade. Especially if you buy the marinade ready-to-use, you couldn't ask for a more instant show-stopper!*

## Makes 4 servings

2 red bell peppers

1 large red onion

$^1/_4$ cup fajita marinade

4 baked potatoes

1 Slice the peppers and onions and put them in a bowl.

2 Toss the vegetables with the fajita marinade. Let stand for 15 minutes.

3 Heat a sprayed nonstick frying pan (or use 2 tablespoons vegetable oil) over medium heat. Sauté the pepper and onions until tender, stirring occasionally.

4 Slit open each potato and squeeze the sides until the potato pushes open.

5 Set the potato halves on a serving plate, spoon the hot vegetables over them, and serve.

Congratulations! You've stocked up with pre-made salsa, yogurt, and fajita marinade—you're prepared for anything potato now! Give yourself a break and take a nap—you deserve it!

The Lazy Way

# Mashed Potato Cakes

*These are so easy it's almost unbelievable! Their mild flavor makes them a great partner for some of your zestier dishes, without having to worry about them causing a flavor-clash! If you think ahead, you can make some extra to bring for lunch the next day. Just warm them up in the microwave, and you'll be the envy of the lunchroom!*

## Makes 4 to 6 servings

3 cups mashed potatoes

Salt, pepper, and garlic powder

1 egg

1 tablespoon olive oil

1 Put mashed potatoes in a bowl and mix in salt, pepper, garlic powder, and the slightly beaten egg.

2 Spray a nonstick frying pan and heat the oil over medium heat.

3 Use a ¼ cup measuring cup to make the potato cakes. Put the potato mixture in pan and shape into a cake using the back of a spatula. Cook the cakes for about four minutes or until golden. Spray the top of the cakes lightly with a butter-flavored, nonstick cooking spray. Turn and cook until the other side is golden, about three to four minutes.

4 Place the cakes on a dinner plate and serve with the ratatouille, salsa, or yogurt.

## A COMPLETE WASTE OF TIME

**The 3 Worst Things You Can Do When Pan-Frying Potatoes:**

1. Don't use a nonstick or coated pan.

2. Use a heavy oil spray (it will take away from the potato).

3. Overcook them.

# Sweet Potato Wedges

*Sweet potatoes are great because they come preflavored, and they add a unique touch to any meal, be it a buffet, picnic, or sit-down dinner.*

**Makes 4 to 6 servings**

4 medium sweet potatoes
Salt, pepper, garlic powder, and dried rosemary to taste
1 cup chunky salsa

1 Preheat oven to 425°F.

2 Wash potatoes and cut lengthwise into wedges, about six wedges to a potato.

3 Soak potatoes in cold water to cover for 10 minutes, then drain. Pat potatoes dry with paper towels.

4 Spray potatoes (or toss with 3 tablespoons olive oil) with a nonstick cooking spray, then sprinkle with salt, pepper, garlic powder, and rosemary. Arrange potatoes in a single layer on a sprayed cookie sheet.

5 Bake potatoes for 45 minutes or until fork tender, turning them with a spatula every 20 minutes. Potatoes will brown and be crisp. Serve hot with salsa for dipping.

YOU'LL THANK YOURSELF LATER

To make your own salsa, mix together a medium chopped red onion, one large chopped tomato, $1/2$ cup fresh chopped cilantro, 1 cup drained and rinsed black beans, $1/4$ cup lime juice, and salt and pepper.

# Steamed New Potatoes

*If you use fresh parsley, wash, drain, and dry it with paper towels. Chop using a mini-food processor. Store extra parsley in a small self-sealing plastic bag.*

## Makes 4 to 6 servings

24 new potatoes

$1/2$ cup Russian dressing or red-wine vinegar dressing

2 tablespoons dried parsley

1 Position the potatoes on a steamer rack above hot water. Cover the pot tightly and continue steaming until the potatoes are done, about 15 minutes. Potatoes are cooked when they can easily be pierced with tip of a knife. Remove the cover away from you to avoid the steam.

2 When the potatoes are cool enough to handle, remove to a serving bowl. Drizzle with the dressing and sprinkle with parsley. Serve immediately.

# Zucchini, Carrot, and Potato Pancakes

*Cooked pancakes can be stored in the freezer. Pop the frozen pancakes into a toaster or put them on a cookie sheet and bake in a 435°F oven until hot.*

## Makes 6 servings

1 medium zucchini

2 carrots

1 potato

1 medium onion

2 eggs (or $^1/_2$ cup egg substitute)

Salt and pepper

$^1/_3$ cup all-purpose flour

1. Grate zucchini ($1^1/_2$ cups) and put it in a bowl. Peel and grate the carrots (1 cup), potato ($1^1/_2$ cups), and onion ($^1/_2$ cup).

2. In a mixing bowl, toss the carrots, potato, and onion with the zucchini. Mix in the egg substitute, salt, pepper, and flour. Let the mixture stand for 20 minutes.

3. Heat a sprayed nonstick frying pan (or use 2 tablespoons butter) over medium heat. Spoon the pancake mixture into the pan, using 3 tablespoons of batter for each pancake. Cook three or four minutes until the pancakes are firm and golden on the bottom. Turn pancakes over and cook until golden. Repeat, using all of the batter and more butter as necessary.

4. Serve hot. Serve the pancakes with applesauce, plain yogurt, or sour cream.

Congratulations! You've made great friends with the world of the spud! Go grab a cup of coffee and take a break!

The Lazy Way

# Hashed Brown Potatoes

## Makes 4 servings

2 or 3 large baked Maine or Idaho potatoes

Salt and pepper

2 or 3 tablespoons vegetable oil

1 Grate the potatoes using a food processor. Season them with salt and pepper.

2 Heat the oil in a nonstick frying pan over medium heat. Add the potatoes in a single layer and flatten them slightly. Continue cooking, over medium-high heat, uncovered for about seven minutes. Do not stir.

3 When the potatoes are browned on the bottom, sprinkle the remaining oil over the top and flip the potatoes. They will break up slightly. Continue cooking for about three minutes until golden. Serve hot.

# Sweet Potato Quesadillas

*Spice mixes such as five-spice mix, chili powder blend, and pumpkin pie spice mix are an invaluable help to the lazy cook, so don't overlook these premade spice combos!*

**Serves 4**

   1$^1$/₃ cups cooked, drained sweet potatoes

   2 teaspoons pumpkin pie spice

   Four 6- to 7-inch flour tortillas

1 In a bowl, mash the sweet potatoes seasoned with pumpkin pie spice.

2 Spoon $^1$/₄ cup of the sweet potato off center on each tortilla and fold in half.

3 Spray a nonstick frying pan (or use 2 tablespoons of butter) over medium heat. Pan-fry the quesadilla about 30 seconds on each side. The tortillas will color slightly and cook quickly.

4 Set a hot quesadilla on each plate and serve. Good with plain yogurt or salsa.

**QUICK ⬭ PAINLESS**

Be sure to use canned sweet potatoes instead of peeling, slicing, and cooking. What a treat for you— no messy preparation!

# Getting Time on Your Side

|  | The Old Way | The Lazy Way |
|---|---|---|
| Cooking sweet potatoes | 25 minutes | 0 minutes (buy them canned) |
| Peeling and slicing potatoes | 20 minutes | 0 minutes (buy them peeled and sliced) |
| Use mashed potatoes as the basis for other dishes | 40 minutes | 0 minutes (use leftovers) |
| Grate potatoes | 25 minutes | 20 seconds (use food processor) |
| Making up spice combos | 15 minutes | 0 minutes (buy them premixed!) |
| Ignoring the spud | Always | Never again! |

# Nip It, Dip It, or Skip It: Say Cheese

Charles de Gaulle was fond of asking, "How can a country have a one-party system when it has over 200 varieties of cheese?" Who among us has met a cheese that he or she didn't like?

Cheese has so much versatility, applicability, and variety that it is difficult to introduce this chapter and its recipes. I can only suggest that cheese will enhance every other food type with which you combine it. Most every food not only willingly marries cheese, but it runs down the aisle. Let's put it this way, I have served many pizzas without tomato sauce (Greek style), and my audience raved, but what response do you think I would get without using cheese?

Some of the cheesy recipes in this chapter are:

- Macaroni, Cheese, and Garden Vegetables
- Focaccia Baby Swiss Sandwich
- Grilled Two-Cheese and Tomato Sandwich
- Two Cheese Strata

- Lasagna Rolls
- Cheese Sub Sandwich
- Farfalle with Ricotta
- Pan-Fried Cheese Ravioli

## A COMPLETE WASTE OF TIME

**The 3 Worst Things You Can Do with Cheese:**

1. Not store it correctly.

2. Not have an assortment of cheese on hand for quick meals and drop-in company.

3. Not select from the wide assortment of fresh grated cheeses.

# Macaroni, Cheese, and Garden Vegetables

## Makes 6 servings

1 package macaroni and cheese

1 tomato

$^1/_2$ cup shredded carrots

$^1/_2$ cup grated broccoli

1 Cook macaroni and cheese according to package directions.

2 While the macaroni is cooking, chop the tomato, shred the carrots, and grate the broccoli if you did not buy them prepared.

3 Put the finished macaroni and cheese in a serving bowl. Toss the hot macaroni with chopped tomatoes, carrots, and broccoli.

**IF YOU'RE SO**
**INCLINED**

*The Lazy Way* to make Macaroni, Cheese, and Garden Vegetables is to use a package variety of macaroni and cheese and add some chopped salad-bar vegetables to the finished dish. Then proudly bring it to the table—your diners will never know it was made *The Lazy Way*.

# Focaccia Baby Swiss Sandwich

*Focaccia is a savory bread that complements just about any-thing you could throw at it—so try lots of different things with this versatile food! You could even add some tomatoes and mozzarella and turn it into a personal pizza—the world is your oyster!*

**Makes 4 to 6 servings**

1 focaccia loaf
1 medium red onion
8 slices baby Swiss cheese or to taste

1 Preheat oven to 350°F.

2 Peel and chop the onion.

3 Slice the focaccia horizontally using a serrated knife. Spread the bread with cheese and onion slices. Replace the top.

4 Cover focaccia with foil and bake in the center of the oven for about 5 to 10 minutes or until warm. Uncover and serve.

**IF YOU'RE SO**
*INCLINED*

Substitute slices of smoked cheese or goat cheese. Be creative, and change the cheese to vary the sandwich with almost no effort.

# Grilled Two-Cheese and Tomato Sandwich

*Try using a stove-top grill and add some outdoor flavor while retaining your indoor comfort!*

## Makes 4 servings

2 tomatoes

1 medium red onion

8 slices millet bread or a multi-grain bread

4 slices Swiss cheese

4 slices Gouda cheese

2 tablespoons butter

1 Slice the tomatoes, and peel and slice onion into rings.

2 Make the sandwiches, putting two slices of cheese on each of four slices of bread. Set some tomato slices and onion rings on top. Cover with the remaining slices of bread.

3 Melt butter in a large nonstick frying pan over medium heat. Fry sandwiches about two minutes on each side or until they are golden brown on each side.

4 Set the sandwiches on plates, cut in half, and serve.

Congratulations! You got yourself a stove-top grill and made getting that great grilled taste much easier! Treat yourself to a night of healthy take-out and give everyone a break!

The Lazy Way

Many bakeries, especially those that promise their customers bread that was "baked the same day," may be willing to hand over their end-of-the-day surplus—give it a try; what could be easier?

# Two Cheese Strata

*This is a great treat for brunch, and the best thing is that you can prepare most of it ahead of time!*

## Makes 6 servings

6 slices day-old whole-wheat bread or egg braid bread

$1/2$ pound grated Monterey Jack cheese

6 eggs

$1 1/2$ cups milk

Salt and pepper

1   Spray or butter an eight-inch soufflé dish. Arrange two slices of the bread on the bottom. Sprinkle with $1/3$ of the cheese. Continue until all the bread and cheese have been used.

2   In a blender or food processor, combine the eggs, milk, salt, and pepper. Pour egg mixture over bread and cheese.

3   Cover dish and refrigerate for eight hours or overnight.

4   Preheat oven to 400°F. Remove the cover and bake in the center of the oven for 40 minutes or until strata is puffy and golden. Serve.

# Lasagna Rolls

*This recipe can get messy, but it's also a great recipe to get the whole family in on! The young budding chefs in your house will start to feel like real gourmets once they've tackled this one! Just make sure they tackle the clean-up too!*

## Makes 6 servings

6 plain or spinach lasagna noodles

One 15-ounce container ricotta cheese

One 10-ounce package defrosted spinach

1$^1$/$_2$ cups shredded mozzarella cheese, divided

2 eggs

2 teaspoons dried oregano

One 27-ounce jar spaghetti sauce

1 Cook the lasagna in boiling, salted water for only 10 minutes, then drain.

2 Preheat oven to 375°F.

3 Using a mixing bowl, combine the cheese, well-drained spinach, 1 cup of the mozzarella, and oregano.

4 Spread about $^1$/$_2$ cup of the filling down the length of each noodle. Roll up each lasagna in jelly-roll fashion. Set rolls, edge side up, in a sprayed ovenproof casserole.

5 Spread the sauce over the rolls and sprinkle with remaining cheese. Bake in the center of the oven for 25 minutes or until done.

6 Serve one roll on each plate.

**Congratulations! You wowed your guests with a new take on the traditional lasagna! Treat yourself to a massage—it's time to relax!**

The Lazy Way

# Cheese Sub Sandwich

*There is a whole new world of sandwiches out there besides the traditional ham and cheese! So leave the meat behind and add some real substance to your cheese sandwiches with a great combination of vegetables. You'll wonder why you never did it this way sooner!*

## Makes 4 servings

Four 8-inch individual French bread rolls

$^1/_2$ cup regular mayonnaise

4 romaine lettuce leaves

$^1/_2$ cup pickle relish

8 slices Swiss cheese

8 slices Genoa cheese

1 red onion

2 tomatoes

1 Slice the bread horizontally and leave open.

2 Spread the bottom half of the bread with mayonnaise and add washed and dried lettuce leaf.

3 Spread the relish over the lettuce and set cheese on the sandwich.

4 Peel and slice the onion and tomatoes. Layer the sandwich with onion rings and tomato slices. Serve.

# Farfalle with Ricotta

*Ricotta is one of the most flexible cheeses out there. Its texture makes it perfect for fillings, and its mild, sweet taste lets it bridge the gap between entree and dessert. This cheese is a must-have for your repertoire!*

## Makes 4 servings

12 ounces farfalle (bow ties)

1 large onion

One 28-ounce can seasoned stewed tomatoes, including juice

$1/2$ cup ricotta cheese

$1/3$ cup grated Romano cheese

1 Cook the farfalle in salted water according to the package and drain.

2 While the farfalle is cooking, peel and chop the onion.

3 Heat a sprayed, nonstick frying pan (or use 2 tablespoons vegetable oil) over medium heat. Sauté the onion until tender, stirring occasionally.

4 Add the tomato and liquid and both cheeses. Continue cooking only about one to two minutes or until hot.

5 Put the hot farfalle in a serving bowl and top with the sauce. Serve hot.

**IF YOU'RE SO**
*INCLINED*

For a more intense flavor, add dried basil, oregano, or garlic powder to taste.

# Pan-Fried Cheese Ravioli

*For added flavor, spoon pesto sauce on the bottom of the serving plate. Set the fried ravioli on top, then sprinkle with cheese and capers.*

## Makes 4 servings

One 9-ounce package fresh cheese ravioli

2 tablespoons butter

$^1/_4$ cup grated Parmesan or Romano cheese

3 tablespoons capers, drained

1 Cook ravioli according to the package. Drain and separate the ravioli, putting them on a buttered cookie sheet. Cover until ready to use.

2 Heat the butter in a nonstick frying pan over medium heat. Sauté the ravioli about five minutes or until they're a golden brown on both sides, turning once.

3 Arrange the ravioli on a serving dish and sprinkle with cheese and capers. Serve hot.

## Getting Time on Your Side

|  | The Old Way | The Lazy Way |
|---|---|---|
| Cheese ravioli | 35 minutes (make them) | 0 minutes (buy them) |
| Grate Parmesan or other hard cheeses | 10 minutes | 3 minutes in a processor |
| Slicing cheese | 10 minutes | 3 minutes in a processor or buy sliced |
| Getting fresh bread to go with cheese | 2$\frac{1}{2}$ hours to bake | 0 minutes (buy it) |
| Settling for an almost-good recipe | Often | Never! Just add cheese! |

# Chapter
## twelve

# Hey, Humpty, You Are Up to Bat!

**E**ggs are one of nature's most perfect foods in their versatility and nutrition content. Eggs contain all nine of the essential amino acids; therefore an egg is a complete protein. Eggs also contain cholesterol and vitamins.

Remember a few hints on egg safety: To be on the safe side, do not eat raw eggs, avoid eggs that have a crack, and use eggs within three to four weeks from the date of purchase.

There are so many egg substitutes and egg-white-only products available today that any concerns about egg use in vegetarian cooking should be forever dismissed. The following egg-based recipes are given with every confidence in the scrumptious quality of the result:

- Egg Fu Yung
- Grit Cakes
- Scrambled Eggs

- Barnyard Scrambled Eggs with Mushrooms

- Scrambled Eggs Stuffed in Pita Halves

- Huevos Rancheros

- Egg-White Denver Omelet

- Eggs Poached in Tomato Sauce

# Egg Fu Yung

*Eggs aren't just for breakfast anymore! Take a page from some of the oldest recipes in the world that come to us from the Far East and maximize the flexibility of this wonderful food!*

## Makes 4 servings

2 green onions

2 cloves garlic

7 eggs (or $1^2/_3$ cup egg substitute)

$^1/_2$ cup frozen green peas

$^1/_4$ cup Oriental sauce

1 Chop the onions in a food processor. Mince the garlic or pass it through a garlic press.

2 In a bowl, lightly beat the eggs. Stir in onions and green peas.

3 Heat a sprayed nonstick frying pan (or use 2 tablespoons peanut oil) over medium heat. Using a $^1/_4$ cup measuring cup, spoon the mixture into the pan. Continue until the pan is full.

4 Continue cooking until the pancakes begin to set around the edges and are golden on the bottom. Turn them over using a spatula and continue cooking until they have set.

5 Put the egg pancakes on a serving platter and drizzle with Oriental sauce.

6 Serve immediately.

YOU'LL THANK YOURSELF LATER

When it comes to using roots like ginger and garlic, here are some valuable tips: Buy ginger preminced as it comes already prepared in a jar; additionally, it is not a good idea to chop and store your own garlic because it runs a higher risk of bacterial growth. Shop smart: Buy the commercial variety.

# Grit Cakes

*"Hidden eggs" is a factor when considering how many eggs you consume in a week. Hidden eggs are found in pancakes, breads, pasta, and cakes.*

### Makes 4 servings

1$\frac{1}{2}$ cup unbleached all-purpose flour

$\frac{3}{4}$ cups white hominy grits

$\frac{1}{2}$ teaspoon each salt, baking powder, and baking soda

1$\frac{1}{2}$ cups buttermilk

3 tablespoons butter or margarine

2 eggs

1. In a deep bowl, mix the flour, grits, salt, baking powder, and baking soda.

2. Melt butter in microwave for a few seconds on high, but let it cool afterward to prevent it from cooking the other ingredients on its own. Stir the buttermilk, cool butter, and eggs into the flour mixture. Let the batter stand at room temperature 20 minutes.

3. Heat a sprayed nonstick frying pan (or use 2 tablespoons of butter) over medium heat. Use a $\frac{1}{4}$ cup measure to spoon the batter onto the pan. Cook until the cakes are firm on the bottom and a golden color. Turn once and continue cooking until golden on the bottom.

4. Serve hot with scrambled eggs and chunky salsa.

## QUICK ██ PAINLESS

This is one of those recipes that is good for a Sunday brunch, a lunch, or an evening meal.

# Scrambled Eggs

*It's always good to come back to the basics. You've made scrambled eggs before for breakfast, but what have you really done with them? This is something that you could make every day, with just a little variation, and never feel as if you're in a rut!*

## IF YOU'RE SO
## *INCLINED*

For scrambled eggs with cheese, add $1/2$ cup grated or diced Swiss or Edam cheese when the eggs begin to set.

## Makes 4 servings

8 eggs (or 4 eggs and 1 cup egg substitute)

2 tablespoons skim milk

Salt and pepper

2 tablespoons butter

1 Using a deep bowl, mix the eggs together with the milk. Season with salt and pepper.

2 Heat the butter in a nonstick frying pan over medium heat. Add the eggs and let them cook, stirring occasionally until the eggs set, about two to three minutes.

3 Put the eggs in a bowl and serve.

For those of you watch-
ing cholesterol, use egg
substitutes. They equal
¹/₄ cup to 1 egg.

# Barnyard Scrambled Eggs with Mushrooms

*This recipe uses the word "barnyard" because it is best when you use fresh eggs. Check the date on the egg carton and always buy the freshest eggs possible.*

## Makes 4 servings

1 medium onion
2 tablespoons butter or margarine
8 ounces sliced mushrooms
8 eggs (or 4 eggs and 1 cup egg substitute)
Salt and pepper

1  Peel and slice the onion.

2  Heat the butter in a nonstick frying pan over medium heat. Sauté the onion and mushrooms until tender, stirring occasionally.

3  In a bowl, lightly beat the eggs. Mix in 3 tablespoons of water or milk and some salt and pepper. Pour the eggs over the vegetables. As the eggs cook, gently fold and stir until the eggs are done to taste, about two minutes.

4  Serve.

# Scrambled Eggs Stuffed in Pita Halves

*Add some spice to your life with this recipe! If you want, you can also make the pita halves yourself; check out Whole-Wheat Pita Pesto Pizza in Chapter 6.*

## Makes 4 servings

1 onion
6 eggs (or 3 eggs and $^3/_4$ cup egg substitute)
Salt, pepper, and garlic powder
One 4-ounce can chopped spicy green peppers, drained
4 whole-wheat pita halves

1 Peel and chop the onion.

2 Heat a sprayed nonstick frying pan (or use 2 tablespoons butter) over medium heat. Sauté the onion until tender, stirring occasionally.

3 Slightly beat the eggs and add them to the pan. Stir eggs as they begin to set. Mix in drained green peppers. Season with salt, pepper, and garlic powder. Continue to cook a few minutes until the eggs have set.

4 Spoon eggs into a warm pita pocket and serve.

**IF YOU'RE SO INCLINED**

To warm the pita bread, pop them one at a time into the toaster to warm, or cover them in foil and heat in a 325°F oven for a few minutes.

# Huevos Rancheros

*Use large eggs unless otherwise specified. For extra flavor,
sprinkle the cooked eggs with $1/4$ cup grated Longhorn
cheese.*

## Makes 4 servings

4 eggs

4 corn tortillas

One 15-ounce can refried beans

2 cups salsa

1 Heat a sprayed nonstick skillet (or use 2 tablespoons vegetable oil) over medium-high heat.

2 Crack open each egg and allow it to fall into the pan.
Reduce the heat to medium and fry the eggs for about two
minutes or until the white part is set and yolks are done to
taste.

3 Set a tortilla on each plate and use a spatula to place an
egg on the tortilla.

4 Heat the refried beans in a sprayed nonstick frying pan
over medium-high heat. Spoon hot beans and salsa on the
side and serve.

# Egg-White Denver Omelet

*Use 8 eggs in place of 1 cup egg substitute and the 4 egg whites. The omelet is good with Hashed Brown Potatoes (see recipe in Chapter 10).*

**Makes 4 servings**

1 medium onion

1 cup egg substitute

4 egg whites

2 to 3 tablespoons vegetable oil or canola blend oil

1 cup cooked, diced potatoes

$^3/_4$ cup diced green bell pepper

Salt and pepper

1 Peel and chop the onion. Set aside.

2 Using an electric mixer, beat the egg whites until they're stiff and glossy peaks form. Fold in egg substitute. Reserve.

3 Heat oil in a nonstick frying pan over medium heat. Cook onion until soft, stirring occasionally. Stir in potatoes and pepper, and cook another four minutes.

4 Fold in egg mixture. As the eggs begin to set, turn and fold the eggs over with a spatula. Cut the omelet into slices and put on individual plates. Serve hot.

YOU'LL THANK YOURSELF LATER

When beating eggs, always have them at room temperature for greater volume.

**You can serve sliced avocado or grated Monterey cheese with this dish.**

# Eggs Poached in Tomato Sauce

*This is a deceptively simple but great-tasting recipe. The combination of the tomato flavoring from the salsa and juice with the flavor of the poached egg yolk is simply heavenly! This is a great alternative to the brunch standard of Eggs Benedict and will add some great color to your table as well!*

## Makes 4 servings

3 cups tomato juice

1 cup salsa

4 eggs

1  Mix the tomato juice and salsa in a medium frying pan only large enough to hold 4 eggs. Heat the mixture over medium heat.

2  Crack each egg and slide it into the heated sauce.

3  Poach the eggs until set, only a few minutes.

4  Using a slotted spoon, lift each egg onto a plate. Spoon the tomato mixture around the eggs and serve. Sprinkle with chopped cilantro if desired.

# Getting Time on Your Side

| | The Old Way | The Lazy Way |
|---|---|---|
| Cracking eggs on side of pan | 10 minutes | 5 minutes |
| Cooking hard-boiled eggs for salad | 20 minutes to boil | 0 minutes (use leftovers) |
| Chopping eggs | 15 minutes | 3 minutes (use a food processor) |
| Having the same old eggs for breakfast or brunch | All the time | Never again! (look at all the options out there!) |
| Cooking too many eggs | 10 minutes | 0 minutes (save them as leftovers) |

# Brave New Culinary World

**T**ofu is a naturally produced by-product of soybeans, high in iron and protein, and contains no cholesterol. Tofu is made from curdled soymilk extracted from soybeans, which is then drained and pressed in a process much like cheese making. In fact, tofu looks much like a large block of creamed or feta cheese. If you think of tofu in this way, it quickly becomes a more acceptable and friendly food product.

Tofu is often referred to as chameleon like; its rather bland, slightly nutty flavor is one of its great virtues as it picks up and marries well with the flavors of the foods with which it is cooked.

Tofu is incredibly versatile, as much as any food product on the market today. It can be mashed, diced, or sliced and used in a wide variety of dishes. Soft, aseptic packaged tofu is great for cakes, dressings, sauces, and pasta fillings. Firm tofu works well in soup, stir-fry dishes, and casseroles. Extra-firm tofu makes an excellent addition to salads. Tofu can be fried,

grilled, stir-fried, baked, boiled, etc. Tofu should be one of the strongest weapons in the arsenal of the vegetarian cook. You've heard of Everyman; tofu is Everyfood.

Tofu spoils easily, so refrigerate and use it within a week. If frozen, it can be kept for several months. Once the tofu package is open, change the water it's stored in each day in the refrigerator.

I'll show you some of the many uses of tofu in these recipes in this chapter:

- Scrambled Tofu
- Raspberry Tofu Pudding
- Tofu Veracruzana
- Cornmeal Mush (Polenta) with Tofu
- Tofu with Steamed Potatoes
- Couscous, Tofu, and Currants
- Indonesian-Style Tofu

# Scrambled Tofu

*For many of us, tofu may have seemed just foreign enough that we became squeamish at the thought of eating it, but give yourself—and tofu—a break! It is jam-packed with vitamins and nutrients and has to be the most versatile food out there. What more could a lazy cook ask for?*

## Makes 4 servings

2 cloves garlic

3 green onions

One 12-ounce package firm tofu

$^1/_4$ cup chopped walnuts

2 tablespoons sesame seeds

1 Chop the garlic and green onions in a food processor.

2 Heat a sprayed, nonstick frying pan (or use 2 tablespoons vegetable oil) over medium-high heat. Stir-fry the garlic and onions until soft. Drain the tofu and stir-fry until lightly golden.

3 Spoon tofu into a bowl and sprinkle with walnuts and sesame seeds. Serve.

YOU'LL THANK YOURSELF LATER

**Learn about tofu! It is an Asian product that is becoming popular here in the United States. It is easily digestible and is a rich source of magnesium, iron, protein, phosphorus, and manganese. Also, it provides some riboflavin, thiamin, vitamin B-6, copper, calcium, and zinc.**

## QUICK  PAINLESS

This recipe is not cooked but blended or processed and served. For these recipes, firm, silken, aseptically packaged tofu is used. It comes in 12.3-ounce containers.

# Raspberry Tofu Pudding

*You can substitute strawberries or apricot preserves for the raspberry preserves. Serve with fresh raspberries.*

### Makes 4 servings

$^1/_4$ cup raspberry preserves

2 teaspoons honey

1 teaspoon vanilla

One 12.3-ounce package soft (custard) tofu

1 Use a blender or a food processor and puree the raspberry preserves, honey, vanilla, and tofu.

2 Serve chilled or at room temperature with raspberries, blueberries, or cinnamon toast.

# Tofu Veracruzana

*Veracruz is a city on the east coast of Mexico. If you like your vegetables with more seasoning, add 2 teaspoons of dried oregano.*

## Makes 4 to 6 servings

2 to 3 tablespoons olive oil

3 cloves garlic

1 large onion

2 cups sliced potatoes

1 red or green bell pepper

One 16-ounce can crushed tomatoes, including liquid

One 12.3-ounce package firm, silken tofu

3 tablespoons capers

1 Heat olive oil in a nonstick frying pan over medium heat.

2 Mince garlic or pass it through a garlic press. Peel and slice onion. Sauté the garlic, onions, and potatoes for about four minutes over medium heat. Add the peppers, tomatoes with liquid, and cubed tofu. Simmer, uncovered, for 8 to 10 minutes.

3 Sprinkle with capers and liquid. Serve either plain or over instant brown rice.

## IF YOU'RE SO INCLINED

Remember that all garlic should be peeled before processing, but not every garlic press requires peeling the garlic. Also remember that sliced potatoes are available washed, sliced, and packaged.

# Cornmeal Mush (Polenta) with Tofu

*Corn is a native North American grain, sacred in ancient times for both the Aztec and Mayan civilizations. The first European settlers were shown the secrets of corn and how to cook it, pop it, store it, combine it with other ingredients, dry it, and plant it. Corn has continued to be a most important ingredient in our diet. We use corn syrup, corn oil, ground corn, popped corn, and corn on the cob. The United States is the world's largest producer and exporter of corn and corn products.*

*The very lazy can buy prepared polenta. Mush, you know, is the American name for polenta. Or you could say that polenta is the Italian word for mush. America had corn first.*

## Makes 4 servings

4 cups cold water
1 cup yellow cornmeal
$^1/_2$ cup drained, diced sun-dried tomatoes
Salt and pepper
One 12-ounce package firm tofu

1. In a medium saucepan, add the cold water and whisk in the cornmeal.

2. Bring the mixture to a boil over medium heat, whisking often. Continue cooking over medium-low heat until the mush thickens, about 20 minutes.

3. Cover, reduce the heat to low, and cook about eight minutes longer. The mush will be thick. Stir in tomatoes. Season with salt and pepper to taste.

## QUICK ◼ PAINLESS

To avoid lumps, whisk the cornmeal together with cold water before cooking. This tip works great, so give it a try. It takes about 20 minutes to make polenta, and it is necessary to stir while cooking. But make enough for two meals—this really cuts your time in half. You can warm mush and sprinkle with brown sugar, nuts, and raisins to serve at breakfast.

4 Drain and cube tofu, then stir it into the mush.

5 Spoon the mush into shallow bowls or use as a side dish. You can also mix in a few tablespoons of butter or serve with tomato sauce or mushrooms on top.

YOU'LL THANK YOURSELF LATER

Remember that you can buy good salsa in the supermarket. If you insist on making it yourself, do so the day before serving and prepare extra salsa to give as gifts.

# Tofu with Steamed Potatoes

*Between steaming and stir-frying, this recipe is quick and painless. Just make sure that to be completely lazy you buy precut vegetables and use fresh tofu. If you follow these simple tips, you'll be home free!*

## Makes 4 to 6 servings

One 12.3-ounce package firm, silken tofu

1 large onion

4 cups sliced steamed potatoes

$^1/_2$ teaspoon minced garlic

$^1/_2$ teaspoon ginger

$^1/_2$ teaspoon curry powder

One 10-ounce package peas, defrosted

One 16-ounce can chopped tomatoes, drained

1 Drain and cube the tofu. Peel and slice the onion.

2 Heat a sprayed nonstick frying pan (or use 2 to 3 table-spoons olive oil) over medium heat.

3 Sauté the onion, potatoes, and tofu sprinkled with spice mixture. Stir-fry the mixture until tender.

4 Mix in the peas and tomatoes. Partially cover, heat, and serve.

## IF YOU'RE SO
## *INCLINED*

**Fill the steamer with enough water to come just below the steamer rack. Bring the water to a boil. Reduce heat to medium. Set the scrubbed potatoes on a heat-proof dish on a steamer rack above the hot water. Cover the pot tightly and steam for 15 minutes or until the potatoes fork tender. Remove cover.**

# Couscous, Tofu, and Currants

*This dish is very filling and quite tasty! As with all of our lazy recipes, this takes just a few minutes to prepare, so it's the perfect solution for a last-minute lunch at home.*

## Makes 4 to 6 servings

One 8-ounce package firm tofu

3 cups cooked couscous

1 teaspoon dried thyme

3 teaspoons orange juice

Salt and pepper

$^1/_2$ cup currants, chopped dried figs, or raisins

**IF YOU'RE SO INCLINED**

Substitute instant barley, instant brown rice, or orzo for the couscous. Also you can add $^1/_2$ cup drained chick peas to the couscous.

1 Drain and cube tofu. Cook couscous according to the package.

2 Heat a sprayed nonstick frying pan (or use 2 tablespoons butter) over medium heat. Sauté tofu until it turns light golden brown. Stir in couscous, thyme, juice, salt, pepper, and figs. Sauté a few minutes until hot. Serve immediately.

# Indonesian-Style Tofu

*Looking for something different? Here's your answer! The deli-cate blend of the peanuts with tofu and coconut is heavenly and can seem almost decadent! Who says that your entree or appetizer can't be just as decadent as the dessert?*

## Makes 4 servings

2 cloves garlic

One 12.3-ounce package firm tofu

One 10-ounce package bagged snow peas

2 cups beans sprouts

Salt and pepper

$^1/_2$ cup chunky peanut butter

$^1/_2$ cup coconut milk

1. Pass the garlic through a garlic press. Drain and cube the tofu.

2. Heat a sprayed, nonstick frying pan (or use 2 tablespoons vegetable oil) over medium-high heat. Sauté the garlic, tofu, and snow peas until the tofu begins to color.

3. Arrange washed and drained bean sprouts on a serving dish and top with tofu mixture. Season with salt and pepper.

4. In a small bowl, mix the peanut butter and coconut milk. Drizzle peanut sauce over tofu. You can sprinkle extra chopped peanuts before serving.

# Getting Time on Your Side

|  | The Old Way | The Lazy Way |
|---|---|---|
| Using sauces with tofu | 30 minutes | 0 minutes (you used prepared sauces!) |
| Preparing tofu | 15 minutes | 0 minutes, all done! (you got yours from the salad bar!) |
| Sweating over complex recipes | 15 minutes | 0 minutes (keep it simple with tofu!) |
| Make a meal out of a salad | 20 minutes | 5 minutes (you just added tofu!) |
| Being afraid to use tofu | All the time | Never again! |
| Recommending tofu | Never | All the time! |

# Now the Real (M)Eat of the Matter

**I**t's where we got our name—vegetarians. Even more than fruits, vegetables run the gamut of tastes, textures, vitamin and mineral content, cooking methodologies, and cooking uses from acorn squash to zucchini.

Vegetable dishes will provide you with an infinite variety of meal possibilities and combinations, and you would have to far exceed Methuselah to wear out or even repeat your vegetable dish repertoire. The recipes in this chapter explore various delicious approaches to the use of vegetables in your cooking. Do not hesitate to experiment, adapt, create, and invent new uses for the world of vegetables.

- Fried Rice
- Baked Eggplant
- Portobello Sandwich
- Taco Platter
- Stir-Fry Veggies with Tempeh

- Asian Coleslaw

- Spinach Pie

- Warm Cauliflower Topped with Cheese and Hazelnuts

## A COMPLETE WASTE OF TIME

**The 3 Worst Things You Can Do with Vegetables:**

1. Not buy processed vegetables, but wash and slice them yourself.

2. Overcook them—no one will eat them.

3. Serve vegetables at the wrong temperature—who would eat cold vegetables when they should be hot?

# Fried Rice

By using brown rice, you add a rich, nutty flavor to the dish. Brown rice also has the bran coating intact. It is a good choice because it is rich in magnesium, phosphorus, and selenium and is a source of vitamin B-6, dietary fiber, thiamin, and niacin. Brown rice takes longer to cook than white rice, but instant brown rice is available and is ready in 10 minutes, stove to table.

For extra protein, incorporate two lightly beaten eggs and/or 1 cup diced tofu when stir-frying.

YOU'LL THANK YOURSELF LATER

The leftover cooked rice should be frozen and used directly from the freezer, thus making it a perfect dish for the lazy cook.

## Makes 4 servings

4 green onions

3 cups instant brown rice

1 medium carrot

2 cups fresh bean sprouts, rinsed and drained

One 10-ounce package green peas

3 tablespoons soy sauce

1 Chop the green onion, grate the carrot, and cook the rice according to the package.

2 Heat a sprayed nonstick frying pan over medium-high heat. Stir-fry the green onions until tender, about three minutes. Mix in the rice.

3 Add the carrots, bean sprouts, and green peas, and stir-fry until hot. Serve.

# Baked Eggplant

## Makes 4 servings

1 large eggplant
1 cup Italian salad dressing
$^{3}/_{4}$ cup grated Romano or Asiago cheese

1   Wash and cut the eggplant into $^{1}/_{2}$-inch slices.

2   Put the eggplant in a shallow glass dish. Cover with salad dressing and marinate for 10 to 20 minutes. Drain.

3   Preheat the oven to 450°F.

4   Set the eggplant on a sprayed, nonstick cooking sheet. Bake in the center of the oven for 20 minutes or until firm, yet translucent.

5   Place the eggplant on a serving dish and sprinkle with cheese and serve.

# Portobello Sandwich

*The beauty of a truly lazy recipe is that it is already working to make yet another recipe painless, so as you remove the stems from the portobellos, freeze them to use later in vegetable soup stock.*

## Makes 4 servings

4 large whole portobello mushroom caps
$^1/_2$ cup Balsamic vinegar salad dressing
4 slices whole-wheat bread

1 Wash the mushroom and peel back the top layer if necessary. Pat dry with paper towels.

2 Arrange mushrooms, face up, in a glass pie plate. Sprinkle them with dressing. Cover and marinate for one to two hours at room temperature or overnight in the refrigerator. Drain.

3 Broil or grill mushrooms for three minutes on each side or until they are firm to the touch, but not mushy.

4 Toast the bread as the mushrooms cook. Arrange a slice of toast on each plate and set one mushroom on top of each slice. Cut the bread in half and serve warm. Decorate with chopped cilantro or sprinkle with rosemary.

**QUICK PAINLESS**

Choose a premade salad dressing from the large assortment available in supermarkets.

# Taco Platter

*This dish is like eating an open-face taco. You can garnish the plate with sliced black olives and sour cream.*

**Makes 4 to 6 servings**

1 small head iceberg lettuce

3 cups tortilla chips

One 15-ounce can kidney beans

1 ripe avocado

2 tablespoons fresh lime juice

3 hard-cooked eggs

2 tomatoes

$^1/_3$ cup vinegar and oil salad dressing

$^1/_4$ pound (1 cup) shredded Cheddar or Monterey Jack cheese

1 Wash and tear the lettuce. Arrange lettuce on a serving platter. Top with tortilla chips and drained kidney beans.

2 Peel and slice the avocado. Brush the avocado slices with lime juice and arrange them on top of the chips and beans. Peel and slice the eggs and arrange on top of the avocado slices. Quarter the tomatoes, and set them on the platter.

3 Drizzle dressing over the salad and serve.

YOU'LL THANK YOURSELF LATER

**The only thing to cook in this recipe are the eggs. Use canned beans, buy the lettuce all washed and torn, and buy the cheese grated.**

# Stir-Fry Veggies with Tempeh

*Tempeh is a high-protein soy food and is so lazy to prepare. It can be sautéed, fried, stewed, grated, or baked. In this recipe it is stir-fried along with the vegetables. Depending on where you live and shop, different varieties of tempeh may be available to you, such as millet, brown rice, and barley. Cover and store tempeh in the refrigerator.*

**Makes 4 servings**

2 tablespoons vegetable oil, divided

One 8-ounce package tempeh

4 green onions

1 bok choy

1 $^{1}/_{2}$ cups snow peas

Salt, pepper, and garlic powder

3 tablespoons Oriental stir-fry sauce

1 Heat 1 tablespoon of the oil in a nonstick frying pan over medium-high heat. Dice the tempeh and stir-fry until it's golden and beginning to crust. Transfer to a plate.

2 Wash and chop the onions and bok choy. Wash and trim the snow peas.

3 Heat the remaining oil and stir-fry the onions, bok choy, and snow peas about five minutes. Season with salt, pepper, and garlic powder. Return the tempeh to the pan and stir in sauce.

4 Serve hot. Good with instant brown rice or buckwheat noodles.

**IF YOU'RE SO**
*INCLINED*

Don't waste the various uses of tempeh; give it a few auditions in your favorite dishes (it goes with just about everything!) and see how much more people go back for—you might be surprised!

# Asian Coleslaw

*"The time has come," the walrus said,*
*"To talk of many things:*
*Of shoes—and ships—and sealing wax—*
*Of cabbages—and kings—"*

*—Lewis Carroll,* The Walrus and the Carpenter

When the time comes to talk of cabbage, which, if your family is like my family, is not very often, the topic usually focuses on coleslaw, that ubiquitous participant at every American picnic, potluck, carry-in event, and grill dinner.

Coleslaw has as many ingredients and variations as there are cooks. Everyone seems to possess a family recipe for coleslaw. However, the basic element of coleslaw has only two possibilities—shredded red or white cabbage. The subsequent ingredients may consist of any combination of the following: chopped onion, celery, sweet green or red peppers, pickles, and herbs mixed with mayonnaise, vinaigrette dressing, and even the addition of some vanilla ice cream. The slaw may be sweet, tart, or tangy.

For those of you watching your cholesterol, you can easily use low-fat mayonnaise or low- or nonfat yogurt as the dressing base.

**Makes 6 to 8 servings**

## For the slaw:

6 cups shredded green cabbage

2 carrots

1 medium red onion

2 teaspoons celery seeds

## For the dressing:

$^3/_4$ cup regular mayonnaise

$^1/_4$ cup white-wine vinegar or tarragon vinegar

3 tablespoons sugar

$^3/_4$ teaspoons salt and garlic powder

$^1/_4$ teaspoons white pepper

1 Put shredded cabbage in a large glass salad bowl.

2 Grate the carrots, and peel and slice the onion. Toss carrots and onion together with the cabbage.

3 Using a small bowl, mix together the remaining ingredients. Stir the dressing with vegetables. Cover and refrigerate until serving time. Stir slaw again before serving. Adjust the seasonings to taste.

YOU'LL THANK YOURSELF LATER

**Buy cabbage and carrots shredded at the produce counter.**

# Spinach Pie

*Spinach isn't just for Popeye, and your kids may decide to give it another whack when they see it prepared like a pie— what's not to love?*

1 prepared pie crust
Two 10-ounce packages frozen chopped spinach, defrosted
8 ounces ricotta cheese
2 eggs
Salt, pepper, and dried dill
Bread crumbs

1 Preheat oven to 350°F.

2 Bake the crust in center of the oven for five minutes. Remove it from the oven.

3 Meanwhile, put the wet spinach in a saucepan, cover, and cook for about two minutes. Cool and squeeze dry using paper towels.

4 Put cheese in a bowl and mix in spinach. Slightly beat the eggs. Mix in eggs, salt, pepper, and dill seeds. Sprinkle with bread crumbs.

5 Spoon mixture into the pie plate. Bake in center of the oven for 45 minutes. The crust will be golden, and the pie will test done when a tester inserted in the center comes out dry.

6 Serve warm with a dollop of sour cream or yogurt.

YOU'LL THANK YOURSELF LATER

**Spinach is rich in iron as well as vitamins A and C.**

# Warm Cauliflower Topped with Cheese and Hazelnuts

*". . . The peach was once a bitter almond; cauliflower is nothing but cabbage with a college education."*
—Mark Twain

YOU'LL THANK YOURSELF LATER

**This is an updated version of an old recipe. You can eliminate or change the nuts to your favorite selection.**

## Makes 4 to 6 servings

1 pound package frozen cauliflower

3 tablespoons butter at room temperature

$1/4$ cup flavored bread crumbs

$1/4$ cup chopped hazelnuts or walnuts

$1/2$ cup grated Cheddar cheese

1 Set the cauliflower in a sauce pan and cook according to package directions, then drain. It should be tender but not mushy.

2 Preheat oven to 350°F.

3 Meanwhile in a small bowl, mix the butter, crumbs, and nuts together.

4 Put the cauliflower in a shallow baking dish. Sprinkle with crumb mixture and grated cheese. Bake in the center of the oven for about seven minutes or until golden brown. Serve hot.

## Getting Time on Your Side

| | The Old Way | The Lazy Way |
|---|---|---|
| Grating cabbage | 20 minutes | 0 minutes (buy it grated) |
| Slicing mushrooms | 10 minutes | 0 minutes (buy them grated) |
| Put together dressings | 10 minutes | 0 minutes (buy them prepared) |
| Using vegetables | 15 minutes, washing, peeling, and slicing | 0 minutes (use frozen) |
| Making coleslaw | 30 minutes | 5 minutes |
| Throwing away leftover vegetables | All the time | Not anymore! |

# Not Rabbit Food, Just Good Habit Food: Salads and Breads

**S**alads were once considered a side dish to a meal. Today, happily, that is not the case, and salads can be complete meals. And terrific, satisfying, colorful, and delicious meals at that!

The nature of the salad has undergone a radical evolution. Hot salads have become a major force, and pasta salads sate the appetite and stimulate the taste buds without leaving one feeling like a boa constrictor after a feeding. Salads have become heartier, tastier, more interesting, and much easier to prepare. Salad dressings are lower in fat and calories and higher in taste. Always a refreshing part of any meal, vegetables have begun to take center stage in many diets. With the growth of farmer's markets and interest in fresh, locally grown produce, the availability of fresh vegetables has increased. Lazy, clever cooks take advantage of the very first lettuce, carrots, asparagus, sweet corn, and juicy vine-ripened red and yellow tomatoes of summer.

Terrific freshly baked breads are omnipresent in today's food markets. All the same, I have included a few bread recipes because they are good recipes for the lazy cook, and, honestly, nothing can top the smell of baking bread. Quick breads and muffins will allow you both ease of preparation and one of humankind's finest treasures, the enjoyment of mouthwatering aromas.

- Rice and Wheat Berry Pilaf
- Barley and Mushroom Salad
- Hearts of Palm and Pink Grapefruit Salad
- Greens with Walnuts and Pears
- Orange and Date Salad
- Tomatoes, Cheese, and Basil Salad
- Celery and Carrot Sticks with Blue Cheese Dressing
- Amaranth Cereal Muffins
- Corn Bread with Quinoa
- Lazy, Lazy Biscuits with Honey

## SALADS TO DIE FOR!

What follows are salad recipes you shouldn't even try to live without! Brace yourself as you step into the land of salad as much more than just a side dish!

YOU'LL THANK YOURSELF LATER

**Don't overlook a fruit salad as a light meal. It is a refreshing change and lazy to prepare.**

COOKING VEGETARIAN *The Lazy Way*

# Rice and Wheat Berry Pilaf

*For extra flavor, cook rice in vegetable stock and add 1 tea-spoon of dried, minced parsley.*

**Makes 4 servings**

1 large onion

One 10-ounce package defrosted sliced carrots

2$^1$/$_2$ cups cooked instant brown rice, cooked according to package directions

1 cup cooked wheat berries, cooked according to package directions

Salt, pepper, and dried basil to taste

1 Peel and chop the onion. Set aside.

2 Heat a sprayed nonstick frying pan over medium heat. Sauté the onion and carrots, partially covered, until tender, stirring occasionally.

3 Stir in the rice and drained wheat berries. Season with salt, pepper, and basil. Cook until hot.

4 Serve over salad greens.

*QUICK*  *PAINLESS*

Work more grains into your vegetarian diet by cooking grains, such as wheat berries and wild rice, in double batches and refrigerate or freeze the extra portions. If you have wheat berries in your freezer and leftover brown rice from earlier in the week, this pilaf goes together in no time at all.

**IF YOU'RE SO**
**INCLINED**

For quick-cooking barley, the same directions apply as for regular pearl barley, but you only need to cook it for 10 minutes.

# Barley and Mushroom Salad

*To cook regular pearl barley, combine 1 cup barley in 2³/₄ cups lightly salted water. Bring to a boil, reduce heat to low, cook covered, 40 to 45 minutes or until tender. Stir once during cooking. Uncover and let stand five minutes before serving.*

## Makes 4 servings

1 cup instant (fine) pearl barley
1 medium red onion
¹/₄ cup French salad dressing
2 cups sliced mushrooms
¹/₂ cup drained peas

1 In a medium saucepan bring 1 cup of water to a boil over medium heat and cover. Stir in the barley, cover, and cook 10 minutes, stirring once. The barley should be tender, and the liquid should be absorbed.

2 While the barley is cooking, peel and chop the onion.

3 Fluff the barley into a salad bowl. Add the onion and mushrooms. Toss salad with the dressing.

4 Serve the salad warm or at room temperature.

# Hearts of Palm and Pink Grapefruit Salad

*Again, the lazy cook knows how to shop! I've told you about the advantages of the salad bar for precut vegetables, but don't forget about your fruits! You can get presectioned grapefruits in the same place!*

**Makes 4 servings**

1 medium head romaine lettuce

One 14-ounce can hearts of palm, drained, and cut in quarters

1 medium red onion

$^1/_2$ cup sweet Russian salad dressing

$1^1/_2$ cups red grapefruit sections, or to taste

1 Wash, dry, and tear the lettuce, or buy it all done for you.

2 To assemble the salad, first arrange the lettuce on salad plates. Sprinkle the hearts of palm evenly on top.

3 Peel and slice the onion. Set onion rings, hearts of palm, and grapefruit segments over the lettuce. Sprinkle salad with dressing and serve.

## IF YOU'RE SO INCLINED

If you have the time and want to make your own Pink Grapefruit Dressing, whisk together $^1/_3$ cup olive oil, $^1/_4$ cup pink grapefruit juice, $^1/_2$ teaspoon each minced garlic and sugar, 3 tablespoons minced fresh parsley, salt, and pepper.

**Buy candied walnuts or pecans, and, naturally, buy the lettuce already washed and torn in pieces. If you have to sweeten your own nuts, spread nuts in a single layer on a nonstick cookie sheet. Sprinkle with sugar. Bake at 250°F for two to four minutes.**

# Greens with Walnuts and Pears

*Pears are an amazing fruit—sweet as you would expect, but with an underlying, heartier punch that blends well will with nuts and vegetables.*

## Makes 4 servings

2 large ripe Bosch pears

6 cups torn salad greens

2 cups sugared walnut or pecan halves

1 cup crumbled blue cheese

$^1/_3$ cup balsamic vinegar salad dressing

1 Cut, core, and slice the pears.

2 Put washed and drained greens in a salad bowl.

3 Mix greens with pears, walnuts, and blue cheese. Toss the salad with dressing.

4 Serve chilled.

# Orange and Date Salad

*Substitute two peeled, seedless oranges for the canned mandarin oranges. Save the orange peel in the freezer. Just mince, on a minute's notice, in a mini-processor and use it to add lots of easy flavor to many dishes from soups to desserts. You can sprinkle this salad with a few tablespoons of minced orange peel and wow your guests.*

## Makes 4 servings

- 1 large head radicchio or other lettuce
- 2 green onions
- One 11-ounce can mandarin oranges, drained
- 1 cup stoned dates
- $^1/_2$ cup olive and vinegar dressing
- Salt and pepper

1 Wash, drain, and roughly tear the lettuce and put it in a salad bowl.

2 Chop the onions in a food processor and add them to the bowl. Toss the lettuce and onions with oranges, dates, dressing, salt, and pepper.

3 Serve chilled or room temperature.

## QUICK ⬤ PAINLESS

You can buy any number of commercial salad dressings that are excellent. If you want to make your own, whisk together $^1/_3$ cup olive oil, 3 tablespoons red-wine vinegar, 1 teaspoon prepared mustard, 2 tablespoons chopped fresh parsley, salt, and pepper.

# Tomato, Cheese, and Basil Salad

*This definitely wins the title of "The Laziest of All Salads!" If you want to give yourself a special treat, add some fresh basil or cilantro. You'll find it was well worth the money when you sample its wonderful flavor and taste.*

*Tomatoes are my personal vegetable favorite, and I am very fussy about the quality of tomatoes served at home. In the summer, tomato plants are planted with regularity. No extra care necessary, just plant and enjoy the tomatoes. When fresh tomatoes have to be bought at the store, spend the extra money and buy only the best.*

*Another variation to try: Add $^1/_2$ cup chopped and drained sun-dried tomatoes to the salad.*

## Makes 4 servings

2 large tomatoes
6 ounces buffalo milk mozzarella cheese
$^1/_2$ cup crumbled goat cheese
$^1/_2$ cup olive oil
$^1/_2$ cup red vinegar dressing
$^1/_4$ cup fresh basil

1 Wash, slice, and arrange the tomatoes on a serving plate.

2 Slice and arrange the mozzarella cheese over tomatoes. Sprinkle the salad with goat cheese.

3 Wash, dry, chop, and sprinkle the basil over the salad. Drizzle with dressing.

4 Serve salad chilled or at room temperature.

# Celery and Carrot Sticks with Blue Cheese Dressing

*Season with salt and pepper if desired.*

## Makes 4 servings

2 large carrots

4 stalks celery

$^1/_2$ cup blue cheese dressing

$^1/_4$ cup capers

1 Wash, peel, and julienne the carrots in a food processor; drain the capers.

2 Julienne the celery. Set the celery on a serving plate with carrots. Sprinkle with salt, pepper, blue cheese, and capers.

3 Serve the salad chilled or at room temperature.

### IF YOU'RE SO
# INCLINED

**Buy the celery and carrots washed, cut, and packaged. They come all prepared in the produce department. Store vegetables in the refrigerator until you need them.**

## PLEASE SIR, CAN I HAVE SOME MORE BREAD?

You've done it—walked past a bakery and felt energized just from the smell of the freshly baking bread products on the other side of that door. It can almost give you a new lease on life! Well, no kitchen would be the same without that smell every so often, so here are a few favorite recipes!

# Amaranth Cereal Muffins

*If you prefer domed muffins, fill the paper cup almost to the top with batter. You will have fewer muffins, but they will be higher.*

*Muffins are among the laziest goodies to make: just lightly mix enough to moisten the ingredients, pour, and bake. For the very, very lazy, use a muffin mix and add raisins or nuts.*

### Makes 10 to 12 muffins

1³/₄ cups amaranth cereal flakes

1 cup whole-wheat flour

¹/₃ cup light brown sugar

1 tablespoon baking powder

1¹/₄ cups milk

2 eggs

3 tablespoons vegetable oil

1 Preheat the oven to 400°F. Set paper liners in a muffin pan.

2 Using a bowl, add the amaranth flakes, flour, sugar, and baking powder. Lightly mix in the milk, eggs, and oil. Add 1 cup of raisins or chopped nuts if desired.

3 Spoon the batter into the muffin pan, filling $^3/_4$ of the paper liners. Bake in the center of the oven for about 20 minutes or until the muffins are firm to the touch or until a tester inserted in the middle of a muffin comes out dry.

4 Cool five minutes, remove from the pan, and serve warm.

**IF YOU'RE SO**
*INCLINED*

Add $^1/_2$ to $^3/_4$ cup chopped figs, dates, apricots, dried cranberries, or nuts to the batter. "Chop" the dates or apricots with kitchen scissors.

# Corn Bread with Quinoa

*Corn bread is a good recipe for a lazy cook. Barely mix all the ingredients together and bake. Or for the very lazy cook, use a corn bread mix—they are very good.*

*Add ¹/₂ cup corn kernels or chopped red bell pepper to the batter for extra flavor.*

## Makes 8 servings

1 cup yellow cornmeal
¹/₂ cup quinoa flour
¹/₂ cup all-purpose flour
¹/₂ teaspoon salt
1 cup whole milk
1 egg
3 tablespoons vegetable oil

1 Preheat the oven to 375°F. Grease or spray an eight-inch baking pan with nonstick cooking spray.

2 Using a mixing bowl, combine the cornmeal, quinoa flour, all-purpose flour, and salt until fluffy. Mix in the milk, egg, and oil. Do not over-beat or your cornbread will be too dense and heavy.

3 Spoon the batter into the pan. Bake the cornbread in the center of the oven for 20 minutes until it is firm or until a tester inserted into the center comes out dry. Cool bread in the pan.

4 Cut bread and serve, cold or warm.

# Lazy, Lazy Biscuits with Honey

*Another great food item that is as good for breakfast as it is with dinner or even as a snack all on its own, the biscuit is indispensable!*

**Makes 10 biscuits**

- 8 tablespoons (1 stick) butter or margarine
- 2 cups Bisquick
- 1 cup sour cream

1 Preheat the oven to 350°F. Use paper liners and fit them into a 12-cup muffin pan.

2 In a small saucepan, melt the butter (or microwave, in a bowl, uncovered, for 30 seconds on high), then cool.

3 In a mixing bowl, lightly mix Bisquick, butter, and sour cream together.

4 Using a $1/4$ cup measure, spoon batter into the paper liners.

5 Bake for 12 to 15 minutes. Muffins will be a golden brown and test done. Serve warm with honey.

## QUICK 🔲 PAINLESS

The honey flavor is derived from the flower from which the nectar was taken. The darker the color, the stronger the flavor.

## Getting Time on Your Side

|  | The Old Way | The Lazy Way |
|---|---|---|
| Making a green salad | 20 minutes | 5 minutes |
| Making a salad lunch | 15 minutes | 5 minutes (stuff it in a pita) |
| Making a double batch of coleslaw | 30 minutes | 0 minutes (it's all done) |
| Keeping salads simple | 45 minutes | 20 minutes |
| Sectioning grapefruit | 15 minutes | Done! (buy presectioned!) |
| Shredding cabbage | 10 minutes | Done! (buy shredded!) |

# Final Temptations

**V**egetarians are usually concerned about their health and therefore do not consume lots of sugar. Even so, a vegetarian does eat dessert. Dessert is a privilege of any diet. I can imagine my husband forgoing many things for the benefit of both his diet and his health, but I know and love him well enough not to deprive him the luxury and innocent pleasure of an interesting dessert for his (or my own) meal.

The dessert recipes I'll give you in this chapter are:

- Cookie Dough Mix
- Apricot-Walnut Cookies
- Honey Couscous with Dried Fruits and Nuts
- Peach Martha Washington Cake
- Crostata Di Ricotta
- Indiana Buttermilk Pie
- Broiled Pineapple Slices

# Cookie Dough Mix

*You can divide the cookie mix into 4-cup sections and store it in plastic bags or containers. As a general rule of thumb, always mix your dry ingredients together first and then deal with the liquids. This recipe is a simple but basic recipe for cookie dough. Make a large batch of it and freeze what you don't need now so you can always have some on hand.*

### Makes 12 cups cookie mix

8 cups self-rising flour

2 cups packed light brown sugar

2 cups granulated sugar

$^{1}/_{2}$ cup water

$1^{1}/_{2}$ cups shortening

1 Divide the ingredients in half and make the dough in two batches using a food processor or a deep bowl and a whisk.

2 First mix the flour and sugars together.

3 Cut or pulse in shortening until the mixture resembles coarse cornmeal.

4 Divide dough in airtight containers and refrigerate or freeze.

**IF YOU'RE SO**
**INCLINED**

Make your cookie dough, refrigerate in an airtight container, and store it for up to one month. The dough is ready for a rainy day or last-minute company.

# Apricot-Walnut Cookies

*Substitute the chopped apricots with raisins, dried pineapple, or raspberry jam.*

*Dried apricots are pitted, unpeeled apricot halves that have a large percentage of the moisture removed. They are rich in vitamin A and are a valuable source of iron and calcium.*

## Makes about 3¹/₂ dozen cookies

4 cups Cookie Dough Mix (see previous recipe)

1 egg

1 cup chopped, dried apricots

¹/₂ cup chopped walnuts

**1** Preheat the oven to 350°F.

**2** Using a deep bowl, mix 2 cups Cookie Dough Mix with the eggs, apricots, walnuts, and ¹/₂ cup water. Blend in the remaining cookie dough. The dough will combine and become moistened.

**3** Using a teaspoon, drop the dough two inches apart on an ungreased cookie sheet.

**4** Bake in the center of the oven for about 12 to 14 minutes or until the cookies are light brown around the edges.

**5** Cool cookies five minutes and remove to a wire rack to cool completely.

YOU'LL THANK YOURSELF LATER

To "chop" the apricots, simply snip them in quarters using a pair of kitchen scissors.

# Honey Couscous with Dried Fruits and Nuts

*Like pasta, couscous (pronounced KOOS-kous), is made of semolina, but unlike other pasta, it cooks quickly into a light, fluffy mass. Couscous originated in northern Africa, probably around Morocco. Making it by hand is very time-consuming. But couscous comes in instant form and is readily available both in regular or whole wheat.*

*Couscous is good savory or sweetened and served as a dessert.*

## Makes 6 servings

3¹/₂ cups water

2 cups instant couscous

¹/₃ cup warm honey

1 teaspoon ground cinnamon

1 cup chopped nuts (such as walnuts, almonds, or pecans)

1 cup dried fruit (such as candied orange peel, candied ginger, or raisins)

1   In a medium saucepan, Bring water to a boil. Stir in the couscous. Cover the pan tightly and remove it from the heat. Let stand for 5 to 10 minutes, until the couscous has absorbed the water.

2   Put the couscous in a serving bowl and fluff it with a fork.

3   Toss couscous with the honey, cinnamon, nuts, and fruits. Taste. If it needs to be sweeter, add light brown sugar by the tablespoon until it tastes right. Serve warm in shallow bowls.

**QUICK ☰ PAINLESS**

To warm honey, place the opened jar in a microwave and cook on high for 20 to 30 seconds.

# Peach Martha Washington Cake

*A Martha Washington Cake is basically a sponge cake layered with jam and sprinkled with confectioner's sugar. If you like, you can bake the cake from a mix, but this idea is even easier. Buy a sponge cake, pound cake, or angel cake, then slice it, spread it with jam, sprinkle with sugar, and serve with fresh peaches and raspberries.*

**Makes 6 to 8 servings**

1 sponge cake
$1/2$ cup peach or raspberry jam
Confectioner's sugar
2 cups defrosted, sliced, and peeled peaches
2 cups fresh raspberries, optional

1 Cut cake into two equal layers.

2 Place the bottom layer of cake on a serving dish and spread with jam. Arrange peaches on top of the jam. Top bottom layer with the remaining cake layer and sprinkle with confectioner's sugar.

3 Slice and serve with washed and drained berries.

## QUICK ⬤ PAINLESS

Dessert can be the easiest part of the meal; just remember there is nothing as refreshing as fresh fruit and cheese.

We've said it before, we'll say it again: One of the major keys to being a good cook is to store your foodstuffs properly so that they'll be fresh when you're ready to use them! Make sure you read the instructions on the package to learn how each foodstuff needs to be stored and what its maximum shelf life should be!

# Crostata Di Ricotta

*Ricotta cheese is a smooth, creamy cheese that is just slightly grainy. Most American ricotta cheese is made with a combination of whey and whole or skim milk.*

## Makes 6 to 8 servings

1 graham-cracker-crumb crust

4 cups ricotta cheese

3 eggs or $^3/_4$ cup egg substitute

$^3/_4$ cup sugar

$2^1/_2$ tablespoons milk

$^3/_4$ cup chopped candied orange peel

2 teaspoons vanilla

1 Preheat the oven to 350°F. Have the graham-cracker-crumb crust handy.

2 Spoon ricotta cheese, sugar, and milk into a bowl. Mix ingredients until smooth. Mix in chopped orange peel and vanilla.

3 Spoon the mixture into the crust. Bake in the center of the oven for 45 minutes or until the filling is set. Cool on a wire rack. When cool, cover lightly and refrigerate until chilled. Cut and serve.

# Indiana Buttermilk Pie

*Sprinkle the finished pie with ground cinnamon or nutmeg for an extra dash of pizzazz. If you want to, you can use egg substitute instead of eggs for this recipe.*

## Makes 6 to 8 servings

- 1 prepared, deep-dish nine-inch pie crust, at room temperature
- 4 tablespoons butter, at room temperature
- $1^1/_2$ cups sugar
- 6 eggs or $2^1/_2$ cups egg substitute
- $^1/_4$ cup all-purpose flour
- 2 cups buttermilk

1 Preheat oven to 300°F.

2 Using a large mixing bowl, whisk together the butter and sugar. Whisk in the eggs. Blend in the flour and buttermilk.

3 Pour the filling carefully into the pie crust. Set pie in the center of the oven and bake 40 minutes or until the pie tests done.

4 Serve warm or cold.

**IF YOU'RE SO**
*INCLINED*

Use prepared pie crusts. They come frozen or in the refrigerator section of the grocery store. They cut cooking time almost in half. You make the filling. Bake and serve.

# Broiled Pineapple Slices

*This recipe marries the tangy pineapple with sweet honey and then throws in juice and nuts. Not only is it delicious to eat, but it can also be beautiful to present!*

## Makes 6 servings

1 large, precored and presliced pineapple
  (about $2^3/_4$ to 2 pounds)

$^1/_4$ cup honey

3 tablespoons frozen orange juice concentrate, thawed

$^1/_3$ cup chopped macadamia nuts or walnuts

1 Using prepeeled and precored pineapple, cut the pineapple into 10 $^1/_2$-inch slices.

2 Set the pineapple slices on a sprayed broiler pan. Preheat the broiler.

3 In a small bowl mix together the honey and orange juice concentrate. Brush the pineapple with the honey mixture.

4 Broil the pineapple about six inches from the heat source for three minutes on each side.

5 Set the pineapple on individual plates and sprinkle with nuts. Serve.

## Getting Time on Your Side

|  | **The Old Way** | **The Lazy Way** |
|---|---|---|
| Making a pie crust | 20 minutes | 0 minutes (buy it) |
| Making cookie mix | 15 minutes | 0 minutes (mix is ready) |
| Preparing a sponge cake | 20 minutes | 0 minutes (buy it) |
| Baking two cakes at a time | 30 minutes | 15 minutes (ingredients are ready to bake) |

# It's Time for a Party: Festive Meatless Meals

T he potluck dinner or progressive party began to evolve when hosts and hostesses began thinking, "I want to entertain, but it is so much work, how can we do it in a more reasonable fashion, a *Lazy Way*?"

Many parties have a "guests should help" concept. Most of these parties have "do-it-yourself" themes. For example, a top-your-own pizza party, or bring-your-own chili for a contest, or an old-fashioned ice-cream social, or a baked potato party with toppings, and everyone helps themselves.

Always have trimmings available at your house and stock chips, pretzels, olives, and dips. Don't forget drinks, bottled water, and the paper supplies. For a complete look, garnish food with any of the following items: pickles, hot peppers, and capers. Have crackers or breads and cut vegetables ready to accompany appetizers. Once the house is stocked, go and have your hair done on the day of the party.

The recipes in this chapter are sure to keep you on the ball when it comes time to entertain!

- Warm Grapefruit and Muesli
- Swiss-Style Muesli
- Lime Melon Wedges
- Chocolate French Toast
- Spiced Orange Slices
- Granola Popcorn
- Apple Toss
- Strawberry Shortcake (and I Do Mean "Short")

## BREAKFAST OR BRUNCH

A breakfast or brunch invitation is elegant and classy. Regardless of the implied formality, a brunch is just a glorious way to start a day.

Here's a selection of recipes to use in any combination. Whether simple or elaborate, a brunch should still be a lazy thing to do.

- Menu
  - Warm Grapefruit and Muesli
  - Swiss-Style Muesli
  - Scrambled Eggs
  - Store-bought cake, muffins, or fresh fruit
  - Coffee or tea

# Warm Grapefruit and Muesli

*This recipe, like most of the recipes in this book, can easily be doubled.*

## Makes 6 servings

3 pink or white grapefruits

$^1/_3$ cup dark brown sugar or maple syrup

3 cups muesli or granola

$^1/_2$ cup dried pineapple or apricot pieces

1 Preheat oven to 350°F.

2 Cut each grapefruit in half. Sprinkle each half with sugar.

3 Set the grapefruit halves in individual oven-proof bowls and sprinkle muesli over the grapefruit.

4 Bake the grapefruit for 5 to 10 minutes or until warm.

5 Sprinkle with dried pineapple or apricot pieces and serve.

## QUICK ⊂▭⊃ PAINLESS

Do not section the grapefruit, but rather have a small sharp knife or grapefruit knife for each guest and allow them to cut the grapefruit themselves.

Muesli can be prepared ahead of time and stored in an airtight container. This Swiss breakfast cereal is so good, try it for a snack or a light lunch.

# Swiss-Style Muesli

*Although there is a way to prepare your own muesli, why add more things to do into your already busy morning? You can buy instant muesli at the supermarket and make your life that much more lazy!*

### Makes 4 servings

2 cups old-fashioned rolled oats

$^1/_2$ cup oat bran

$^1/_2$ cup dark or golden raisins

$^1/_2$ cup chopped, dried apricots

$^1/_3$ cup sunflower seed kernels

1 teaspoon ground cinnamon

1 In a large bowl, toss all the ingredients together.

2 Store in a covered container.

## Scrambled Eggs Anyone?

With eggs in the house, you can always make Scrambled Eggs (see full recipe in Chapter 12). They are fun to make and take only minutes to complete. Make scrambled eggs and add a few tablespoons of chopped green onions, tomatoes, or mushrooms.

If you or your friends are watching your cholesterol, you can use an egg substitute. Everyone will feel they are taking care of themselves.

## Coffee Break

Invest in a good coffee pot and good coffee, and you will not be disappointed. The aroma of the coffee will greet your guests as they enter the door.

## WINTER BRUNCH

It's your best friend's birthday, and it's cold and snowy outside. Call and invite him or her over for brunch. It is always a treat to be invited to a friend's house, especially if you are being remembered in a special way.

It is a good idea to have party foods stocked in the pantry. This can include packaged cookies, such as filled cookies, fancy shaped cookies, chocolate cookies, or nut cookies. Take your pick.

Juice has come into it's own. You can serve pear juice, peach juice, any number of blended combinations with cranberry juice, tangerine, guava, and pink grapefruit.

Refer to your pantry as your "store." Have pretty and appropriate paper goods available in your "store." White is a good choice—it's always nice looking. If you prefer something with more color, try flowered napkins

### A COMPLETE WASTE OF TIME

**The 3 Worst Things You Can Do When It Comes to an Impending Party:**

1. Try to do everything yourself.

2. Don't be creative.

3. Don't get your guests in on the act!

and matching plates, and remember to get assorted sizes.

Warm people's stomachs as well as their hearts with these creative recipes:

- Menu

    - Lime Melon Wedges

    - Juice

    - Chocolate French Toast

    - Spiced Orange Slices

    - Coffee and store-bought cookies

# Lime Melon Wedges

*Nothing quite beats the zesty flavor of lime. This is a great treat for those hot summer months!*

## Makes 6 servings

1 medium cantaloupe

$^1/_3$ cup honey, at room temperature

Ground cinnamon

6 lime wedges

1 Peel and cut the melon in wedges. Put the wedges on a serving platter or individual plates.

2 Drizzle honey over the melon and sprinkle with cinnamon. Set a lime wedge on the side for the guest to squeeze over the melon, and serve.

YOU'LL THANK YOURSELF LATER

Be sure the melon is ripe. There is nothing as bad as a dry melon and nothing as great as a juicy, ripe melon. They are low in calories and high in flavor. The melon with the deep orange color has potassium and vitamins A and C.

# Chocolate French Toast

*Everyone will love this new take on an old favorite! You might also try adding a teaspoon of vanilla extract to add to the flavor.*

### Serves 4

4 eggs

1 cup milk

2 tablespoons unsweetened cocoa

2 tablespoons sugar

4 large slices egg braid bread

2 tablespoons butter

1 In a shallow bowl, blend slightly beaten eggs, milk, cocoa, and sugar.

2 Soak the bread in the egg mixture for five minutes on each side.

3 Heat the butter in a nonstick frying pan over medium heat. Pan-fry the toast until golden brown on both sides.

4 Serve toast hot with maple syrup, strawberry syrup, or berries.

Congratulations! You stocked your pantry with some fancy cookies, pretty napkins, and good coffee! You're ready for any special occasion that comes knocking on your door! Now kick back and relax with a steaming cup of coffee!

The Lazy Way

# Spiced Orange Slices

*The cinnamon and cloves in this recipe turn a great-tasting orange into a sinful treat! This will definitely become a new favorite on the block!*

## Makes 6 to 8 servings

5 or 6 large seedless oranges

$^1/_2$ cup orange juice

$^1/_3$ cup light brown sugar

2 cinnamon sticks

8 whole cloves

Port to taste

1 Peel and slice the oranges and put them in a shallow glass bowl.

2 Mix in the orange juice, sugar, and cinnamon sticks. Stick each clove in the center of an orange slice. Cover oranges with Port.

3 Cover and refrigerate up to eight hours or overnight, giving the flavors a chance to blend.

## IF YOU'RE SO
## INCLINED

Make this dish the day or two before serving and let the flavors blend together in the refrigerator. You can add a little red wine to the oranges, if you are so inclined.

# A PIZZA CONTEST

To host a pizza competition, first ask two of your guests to be judges. Have the remaining guests write their names on a sheet of paper. Have the judges consider categories such as shape, design, and creativity. The contestant with the best marks wins. Make sure that you have a prize for the winner.

## Pizza Crust

On a platter, place your prepared pizza crusts (store-bought, and you should know that many pizza restaurants sell their crusts, so look around; you never know). You could substitute regular pizza crust with pita rounds, Boboli, English muffins, focaccia, or other small prepared crusts.

If you want and insist on making your own dough, have the dough in balls so that each guest (contestant) can roll their own crust. At least you won't have to do that, too.

## Topping

Toppings and sauces should be arranged on the table, and contestants should be instructed to create their own pizza. Don't faint when you see this list. Please pick and choose only the toppings that you think fit your crowd. Do not use all of the toppings at one time. You can be simple and elegant and have sauce, a few vegetables, and a few varieties of grated cheese.

- Red pizza sauce
- Spicy grated cheese

- Mild crumbled cheese such as a goat cheese or Colby
- Ricotta cheese
- Sliced tomatoes
- Sun-dried tomato bits
- Sliced or diced peppers
- Sliced onions
- Drained chick peas
- Minced garlic (from a jar, of course)
- Grated Parmesan cheese
- Capers
- Olives
- Fresh cilantro
- Vegetables, such as drained asparagus tips or sliced mushrooms

## Judges

The judges do not eat the pizzas (during the contest at least!), but judge them in several categories:

- Best design
- Best shape
- Most creative

## Guidelines

These guidelines are just a jumping off place for you. Feel free to modify them as you see fit!

1. No entrant can be a judge.

2. It is fun if there is an audience made up of some nonparticipating guests.

## QUICK n PAINLESS

Use plastic bowls to serve the topping options, and your post-party cleanup will be a snap!

3. Take pictures of the winners—someone in the group must have an instant camera—and let someone other than yourself be responsible for the pictures.

4. Set a time limit.

5. The prize to the winner can be a jar of pizza sauce, spirited gifts, or anything you want including, of course, this book!

6. Have a table ready to display pizzas.

7. Contestants can prepare more than one entry.

8. Eat and enjoy the hot pizza. Serve with soda, juice, or beer. Serve fruit for dessert.

The following list will give you some great ideas for hosting your own pizza competition.

- Menu
    - Bruschetta (see recipe in Chapter 6)
    - Pizza (see recipes in Chapter 6)
    - Drinks
    - Fresh fruit

## PIGSKIN PARTY (OR BASKETBALL, LUGE, DOWNHILL SKIING, OR WHATEVER SPORT YOU LIKE)

This will be a long afternoon, so space out serving your food. Encourage guests to cheer and complain about the teams, and then serve food to soothe them. This will work for tailgating or home parties. Have soda and other drinks available, as well as nibbles, bowls of cut veggies

Congratulations! You found some great but inexpensive door prizes for your pizza contest! Relax—now it's time to enjoy the fruits of your guests' labors!

The Lazy Way

(crudités) and store-bought dip, a beautiful arranged cheese tray with crackers, thin-sliced French bread, and large branches of grapes and/or apples and pears. Nachos are also a good choice.

Have some bottled water on hand along with other favorite drinks.

You won't have to slave in the kitchen all day for this type of gathering. Use these menu ideas to get yourself on the ball!

Make sure you have selected toppings that will blend nicely with each other and keep an eye on what people do with them. You just might end up with a host of new menu ideas for next month!

- Menu

  - Granola Popcorn or store-bought popcorn

  - Chili (see recipes in Chapter 7)

  - Cheese Sub Sandwiches (see recipe in Chapter 11)

  - Apple Toss

  - Strawberry Shortcake (and I Do Mean "Short")

# Granola Popcorn

*Start the party with Granola Popcorn, serve chili (there are two recipes to choose from in the appetizer chapter) and/or grinder sandwiches with Apple Toss or Strawberry Shortcake for dessert.*

## Makes 6 to 8 servings

6 cups plain, popped corn

3 tablespoons butter, melted and cooled

3 tablespoons warm honey

3 tablespoons packed dark brown sugar

1 cup old-fashioned oats

$^1/_2$ cup raisins

$^1/_2$ cup slivered almonds

$^1/_2$ cup sunflower seed kernels

1 Preheat the oven to 300°F.

2 Using a large mixing bowl, toss the popcorn with the remaining ingredients.

3 Spoon the mixture into a sprayed 2-quart casserole. Bake the popcorn for 30 minutes, stirring once.

4 Spread the popcorn on a baking sheet to cool, then put it in a bowl and serve.

**IF YOU'RE SO**
*INCLINED*

**To pop your own popcorn put $^1/_2$ cup unpopped corn in a brown grocery or lunch bag (without any writing on it) and seal securely (no staples!). Set the bag in the microwave and cook on high for 3$^1/_2$ to 4 minutes. You will hear the corn stop popping when it is done.**

## Cheese Tray with Crackers and Fruit

Shop at the local cheese shop or cheese area of a large supermarket. Buy old reliable types of cheese, but also experiment and buy a few new ones that everyone can talk about. Goat cheese is a mild favorite; it even comes with flavoring. Serve a basket or tray with at least two types of crackers, party breads, or thin-sliced French bread. Serve the cut vegetables (which you purchased already cut) nearby.

## Chili

There are two chili recipes in the appetizer chapter of this book. And of course—my favorite thought—make it the day before. If you are entertaining lots of people, serve the chili with a tossed salad, from a salad bar of course. An easy compromise is to buy torn lettuce and put it in a bowl. Buy toppings from a salad bar and scatter on top of the torn lettuce. Serve two or three bottled dressings so everyone can choose his or her favorite.

## Cheese Sub Sandwich

Again, arrange food on a tray and encourage your guests to help themselves. Most people think it is fun to help themselves, so give them a chance.

## QUICK ⬤ PAINLESS

For crumbled butter, simply take a cold stick of butter and cut into small pieces. You can also use whipped butter for the same purpose (Land O' Lakes makes it).

# Apple Toss

*Remember to buy the apples all peeled and sliced—look in the refrigerated section of the supermarket.*

### Makes 6 to 8 servings

4 cups sliced and peeled apples

¹/₂ cup all-purpose flour

3 tablespoons butter

¹/₂ cup sugar

1 teaspoon ground cinnamon

1 Preheat oven to 400°F. Spray or grease a 9×9×2–inch baking pan.

2 In a large bowl, toss the apples with the flour, crumbled butter, sugar, and cinnamon. Arrange apples in prepared pan.

3 Bake in the center of the oven for 35 minutes. Apples will be tender.

4 Spoon into sauce dishes and serve warm. Try it with vanilla ice cream on top for a special treat.

# Strawberry Shortcake (and I Do Mean "Short")

*Substitute 2 cups sweetened, whipped, heavy cream for the nondairy cream.*

## Makes 8 servings

1 pint strawberries

$^1/_4$ cup sugar

2-layer sponge cake

One 8-ounce package nondairy topping

1  Wash the strawberries, remove their hulls, and cut in half. Put berries in a bowl and sprinkle with sugar.

2  Put one half of the cake on a serving plate. Cover with cream, and scatter half of the berries over the cake. Replace top of cake over bottom layer. Cover cake with remaining cream. Scatter strawberries over top.

3  Cut the cake and serve. Can it be more lazy?

YOU'LL THANK YOURSELF LATER

**Buy ready-made sponge cakes, and you'll be able to whip out this great shortcake recipe in the blink of an eye!**

## BAKED-POTATO PARTY

The baked potatoes are cooked to perfection, served piping hot with sauces and toppings, and your guests help themselves. Serve a large green salad, and the party is off and running. Be sure to have paper plates and plastic cups available. I prefer real knives and forks to plastic, but choose what is lazy and comfortable for you. With plastic, cleanup is almost nonexistent.

The party has to be fun for you. Make time to pamper yourself before your guests arrive. When some frail voice in the back of the room says, "Let me help clean up," the instant response should be, "Great."

Let's make this party for eight guests. Bake 8 to 10 medium-large scrubbed and poked baking potatoes at 400°F for one hour or until tender. Remove the potatoes, and when they are cool enough to handle, cut lengthwise and squeeze to puff out the sides. Set the potatoes on a tray, garnish with parsley or cilantro, and serve.

### Toppings

Choose only a few from the following ideas:

- Chopped tomatoes
- Chopped red onions
- Chopped green onions
- Sour cream
- Yogurt
- Grated cheese
- Shakers of seasonings, salt, pepper, and paprika

- Garlic powder, dried basil, dried oregano, curry powder, and onion flakes

- Creamed spinach or other greens, available in cans

- Melted cheese (in the microwave)

- Diced tofu

- Drained chick peas

- Heated refried beans

- Mushrooms

- Sliced olives

The following menu items are great for any impromptu gathering, and the ingredients are pretty inexpensive. It's a good idea to have the makings for some of these items on hand all the time so you won't be caught with an empty plate when you have unexpected guests!

- Menu

    - Salsa and corn chips

    - Baked potatoes with do-it-yourself toppings

    - Cookies (see recipes in Chapter 16)

    - Tea, coffee, and select soft drinks

## Salsa and Corn Chips

There are so many prepared salsas on the market, you will have a good time choosing one, two, or three varieties. To add your own touch, add chopped, fresh (from the salad bar) pineapple to a salsa or add a chopped small hot pepper to another.

**A COMPLETE WASTE OF TIME**

The 3 Worst Things You Can Do with Toppings:

1. Don't use your food processor to prepare them.

2. Don't take advantage of your supermarket salad bar.

3. Don't buy them prepared.

## "OLD-FASHIONED" ICE-CREAM SOCIAL

The ice-cream social is such a lazy way to entertain. Try it for Valentine's Day or after a school meeting. Whatever the time or occasion may be, remember that all the food is in the freezer, refrigerator, or pastry box from the local bakery. Once again, I advocate: Let your guests help make the party by helping themselves to the food. Participation by guests is just a joy for the hostess and host.

Usually one does not think of vegetarians as enjoying desserts. The reality is that vegetarians do enjoy desserts, but they are usually health-conscious and therefore stay away from the overly sugared desserts and gravitate to the healthier choices. This party is for that special occasion when you want a very lazy party. The paper supplies for this party will vary slightly because in addition to the plastic cups, small plates for the cookies or cake, napkins, and plastic spoons, you will need paper dessert dishes for the ice cream.

If this party is for a Valentine's Day afternoon, have two flavors of ice cream, probably vanilla and strawberry. If you are a chocoholic, by all means don't omit chocolate—have chocolate ice cream, too. Have a bowl of nondairy topping and sweetened whipped cream, cherries, chopped walnuts or pecans, and chocolate sauce, hot fudge sauce, or strawberry sauce.

Shop around and buy a chocolate sauce that you think is grand. You can also have marshmallow topping. Have lots of spoons available so guests can help themselves.

Congratulations! You've just had your first ice-cream social! Treat yourself to an afternoon in the park with the family!

The Lazy Way

After a while, serve a plate of store-bought cookies or a plain cake, like the Peach Martha Washington Cake, and drinks. Look for a lot of smiling faces.

The following are some great ideas for hosting your own Old-Fashioned Ice-Cream Social!

- Menu

    - Do-it-yourself ice-cream sundaes

    - Peach Martha Washington Cake (see recipe in Chapter 16)

    - Cookies

    - Tea, coffee, or lemonade

YOU'LL THANK YOURSELF LATER

Choose recipes that you can prepare the day before the event, and you'll be that much more relaxed when party day arrives!

## Getting Time on Your Side

|  | The Old Way | The Lazy Way |
|---|---|---|
| Preparing for the party | Hours | 20 minutes |
| Sprinkling toppings on individual plates | 30 minutes | Never again! |
| Sectioning fruit | 20 minutes | Done! (you bought them that way!) |
| Getting caught by surprise with unexpected guests | Often | Never again! |
| Coming up with ways for the guests to bring the party to you | Never | Always! |
| Cleaning up after a party | Hours | 30 minutes (even less when the guests chip in!) |

# More Lazy Stuff

# How to Get Someone Else to Do It

**I** have spent much page space in this book suggesting that you use your friend the produce manager as your out-of-house chef. This is a strong recommendation because most people that you purchase products from will be interested in your behalf. They will care about you. Trust me on this because your satisfaction ensures that they are doing their job well. Also, you will sacrifice a most valuable and irreplaceable asset if you do not use the produce manager to the greatest degree.

However, let's assume you have absolutely no persuasive or friendly powers. Use the following ideas to ameliorate the workload.

## THE VALUE OF A WELL-PLACED FAMILY MEMBER

For goodness sake, let your family assist you. Delegate certain kitchen preparation, cooking, or cleanup chores to various family members. My early memory of helping in the kitchen was that of a reward, not a burden. My mother used positive psychology on me. She would say, "You are now allowed to do certain things in the kitchen," and I was highly flattered and made every attempt to be competent and capable, lest my mother should take my privilege from me.

Other than decorating the Christmas tree, there is no single family event that inspires cooperation like eating. Do not make any chore seem like a "job"—from putting away the dishes, setting the table, emptying the garbage, taking the dishes off the table, or making the salad—make it seem like a contribution, not a chore.

Make every assignment seem like an opportunity to assist in a communal endeavor. If everyone in your family carries out a light, but personally involved task, the overall burden will be diminished by so many degrees of self satisfaction.

## ACCEPTING OUTSIDE HELP

Never decline assistance. If space is limited in your kitchen, devise a route or station where every assisting effort is used to its maximum extent.

When you are entertaining and so-and-so calls with the "What can I bring?" question, never say, "Oh, nothing, I've got it all covered." Instead, respond with, "Bring dessert or a salad, and how nice of you to offer." First of all, you probably don't have it all covered, and everyone will honestly feel better if he or she is allowed to contribute to the overall endeavor.

My husband loves to garnish plates before they are served and to decorate the dining table. I have always treasured this and have saved many hours of time in allowing him to do this little thing. By the way, I have used many of his decoration efforts as suggestions in my cookbooks.

Every child in the house should have his or her own recipe that is made with regularity. The recipe should match the age and interest of the child. Young children can be taught to make a salad dressing, whereas an older child can make the salad. Teenagers enjoy stir-frying recipes, while there is always someone you can teach to make a dessert. Kids love to feel like they are important and that they play a significant role in the life of a family. Never discourage any help on the part of a child, even if it isn't, in fact, help. Always encourage a child to participate to the fullest extent of his ability in the jobs that create meals and family togetherness.

B

# If You Really Want More, Read These

**T**here is certainly no shortage of cookbooks in the land. What is in short supply is time—time to read cookbooks, time to shop, time to prepare food, time to cook, time to clean up the kitchen. In recent years, authors and publishers have begun to address this problem, and now a growing number of handy books are available on how to simplify your life and how to complete onerous chores more easily, speedily, and efficiently—or eliminate them all together. I recommend you obtain every book in *The Lazy Way* series—just think of all the extra time you will have!

Use your library, bookstore, or www.amazon.com on the Internet. Here are just a few of my favorite books:

Emmonds, Didi. *Vegetarian Planet: 350 Big-Flavor Recipes For Out-Of-This-World Food Every Day*. The Harvard Common Press, 1997.

*Famous Brand Name Vegetarian Cooking.* Publications International, Ltd., 1997.

Fritschner, Sarah. *Vegetarian Express Lane Cookbook.* Chapters Publishing, Ltd., 1996.

Grunes, Barbara. *The Complete Idiot's Guide to Grilling*. Alpha Books, 1999.

Grunes, Barbara, and Virginia Van Vynck. *All American Vegetarian*. Henry Holdt Publishers, 1995.

Grunes, Barbara, and Virginia Van Vynck. *All American Waves Of Grain*. Henry Holdt Publishers, 1997.

Havala, Suzanne. *The Complete Idiot's Guide to Being Vegetarian.* Alpha Books, 1999.

Jacobi, Dana. *Soy!* Prima Publishing, 1983.

Jones, Jeanne. *Healthy Cooking for People Who Don't Have Time to Cook*. Rodale Press, 1997.

Lappé, Frances Moore. *Diet for a Small Planet*. Ballantine Books, 1992.

Lo, Kenneth. *Chinese Vegetarian Cooking*. Pantheon Books, 1974.

Mitchell, Paulette. *The Complete Soy Cookbook.* Macmillan USA, 1998.

The Moosewood Collective. *Sundays at Moosewood Restaurant*. Simon & Schuster, 1990.

Spitler, Sue. *1,001 Low-Fat Vegetarian Recipes*. Surrey Books, 1997.

# If You Don't Know What It Means/Does, Look Here

## COOKING TERMS AND MEASURING UP

Did you ever hit a memory block while reading a recipe? Or find yourself standing with a glazed look on your face as you try to remember how many ounces are in a pound? Well we're here to help you avoid that deer-in-headlights feeling! We know you already know all this stuff, but sometimes even the best of us, and definitely the busiest of us, need a little cheat sheet to keep moving forward!

### Cooking Terms

There are basic cooking terms used in this book, and these definitions are here just to refresh your memory.

**Beat**  Stir vigorously using a whisk, spoon, or an electric mixer.

**Blend**  To mix two or more ingredients together until they are smooth.

**Broil**  Cook food by direct, dry heat under a preheated broiler element.

**Chop**  Cut the food into uniform pieces.

**Cream** To beat room temperature (soft) butter or margarine together, usually with sugar, until light.

**Crumble** To break a larger piece of food into smaller pieces with your fingers, as with goat cheese.

**Cube** To cut food into uniform squares.

**Dice** To cut food into small, uniform pieces (usually $1/2$ inch).

**Fold** To combine light, fluffy ingredients, such as beaten egg whites, into a denser mixture with a gentle over and around motion.

**Garnish** To accent the food with a pretty decoration, such as trimmed parsley.

**Grate** To shred into coarse or fine pieces.

**Grease** To coat the inside cooking surface of a pan with a nonstick cooking spray, butter, or margarine to prevent sticking.

**Julienne** To cut food into thin, long, uniform strips, such as a match-stick shape.

**Par-broil** To cook food in water until about halfway done and then removing it from the water.

**Peel** To remove the skin of a vegetable or fruit with a small, sharp knife or peeler.

**Poach** To cook food that's barely covered in simmering liquid that is usually flavored.

**Proof** To let the yeast and water mixture bubble to begin the action of yeast.

**Puree** To process, blend, or press to a smooth texture.

**Reduce** To boil a liquid, uncovered, to lessen the amount of liquid, thereby intensifying the flavor.

**Sauté** To cook food quickly (in a small amount of oil or other fat) in a frying pan on top of the stove.

**Shred** To cup food into small, thin pieces. Shredding is usually done with a grater or food processor.

**Simmer** To cook food over a low heat.

**Skim** To remove any fat forming on the surface of a liquid.

**Slice** To cut in flat pieces of equal size, usually with a food processor or grater.

**Soak** To let stand in liquid, as with beans.

**Toss** To mix by gently turning the ingredients over in a bowl, using a fork and spoon or a salad fork and spoon.

**Whisk** To beat a liquid with a whisk or electric mixer until it is bubbly or stiff.

## Measuring Up

It is always a good idea to have a measuring chart for times when you are doubling or tripling a recipe or just forget, even if only for a moment, the correct numbers. Always use a standard glass measuring cup for liquids and measuring spoons and cups for dry ingredients. Dip and lightly sweep flour, sugar, or other dry ingredients into the cup and level it off with a knife. That pesky shortening can be packed into the measuring cup with the back of a spoon or a small spatula.

# Measurements

| This... | Equals This... |
|---------|----------------|
| 1 tablespoon | 3 teaspoons or $^1/_2$ ounce |
| 2 tablespoons | 1 fluid ounce or $^1/_8$ of a cup |
| $^1/_4$ cup | 4 tablespoons or 2 fluid ounces |
| $^1/_3$ cup | 5 tablespoons plus 1 teaspoon |
| $^1/_2$ cup | 8 tablespoons or 4 fluid ounces |
| $^3/_4$ cup | 12 tablespoons or 6 fluid ounces |
| 1 cup | 16 tablespoons or 8 fluid ounces |
| 1 pint | 2 cups or 16 fluid ounces |
| 1 quart | 4 cups, 2 pints, or 32 fluid ounces |
| 1 gallon | 4 quarts, 8 pints, 16 cups, or 64 fluid ounces |
| 1 pound | 16 ounces |

D

# It's Time for Your Reward

| Once You've Done This... | Reward Yourself... |
|---|---|
| Reorganized your kitchen | Order in dinner |
| Stocked your pantry | Scratch off tomorrow's last-minute rush to the supermarket |
| Introduced yourself to the supermarket produce manager | Treat yourself to a cup of tea or coffee |
| Fed your family on leftovers | Enjoy your favorite TV show |
| Made your food processor do the dirty work | Enjoy a luxurious bubble bath |
| Used prepared foods from the supermarket salad bar | Buy yourself a bouquet of fresh flowers |
| Used tofu | Take the afternoon off |
| Made a menu for next week | Get a facial |
| Hosted a Pizza Contest Party | Go see a movie |
| Got the family in on the act | Go on a family outing |

# Swaps and Substitutions

**S**ure, we'd all love to be one of those super people who always has everything they need when they walk into the kitchen, but let's face it, who really has that kind of time?

The good lazy cook not only tries to be prepared but can also think on his or her feet when they are, inevitably, caught short. Keep these ideas in mind the next time your panic meter starts to rise, and you'll be able to save the day!

## SWAPS TO SAVE YOU

If you are caught short on a rainy day, you can substitute the following ingredients:

| If You Don't Have... | You Can Use... |
| --- | --- |
| 1 teaspoon baking powder | $1/4$ teaspoon baking soda and $1/2$ teaspoon cream of tartar |
| 1 cup bread crumbs | 1 cup cracker crumbs |
| 1 cup buttermilk | 1 cup yogurt OR 1 cup whole milk with 1 tablespoon vinegar |

| If You Don't Have... | You Can Use... |
|---|---|
| 1 ounce (square) chocolate | 3 tablespoons cocoa plus $1\frac{1}{2}$ teaspoons shortening |
| Cottage cheese | Farmer's cheese OR pot cheese |
| 1 tablespoon cornstarch | 2 tablespoons all-purpose flour |
| 1 egg | $\frac{1}{4}$ cup egg substitute |
| 1 cup sifted cake flour | 1 cup sifted all-purpose flour, minus 2 tablespoons |
| Kidney beans | Navy beans, pinto beans, or garbanzo beans |
| Black pepper | White pepper |
| 1 tablespoon chopped fresh herbs | $\frac{1}{2}$ to 1 teaspoon dried herbs |

## YOU WANT HOW MUCH OF WHAT?

We've all gotten frustrated trying to figure out how much of a foodstuff will give the proper measurement for a recipe. Here are a few of my rules of thumb that I use when I need to find a food equivalent for a specific recipe.

| This Much... | Will Give You This... |
|---|---|
| Apples, 1 pound | 3 apples |
| Dried apricots, 1 pound | $2\frac{1}{4}$ cups |

| This Much... | Will Give You This... |
| --- | --- |
| Berries, 1 quart | $3^1/_2$ cups |
| Berries, 1 pint | $1^1/_2$ cups |
| Bread crumbs, 1 slice fresh bread | $^3/_4$ cup soft crumbs |
| Butter, 1 pound | 2 cups |
| Butter, 1 stick | 8 tablespoons or $^1/_2$ cup |
| Cottage cheese, 8 ounces | 1 cup |
| Cream cheese, 3 ounces | 6 tablespoons |
| Cheddar cheese, $^1/_4$ pound | 1 cup shredded |
| Cornmeal, 1 cup uncooked | 4 cups cooked |
| Eggs, 5 medium | 1 cup |
| Flour (all-purpose), 1 pound | $4^1/_2$ to 5 cups sifted |
| Graham crackers, 15 | 1 cup crumbs |
| Lemons, 1 medium | 3 tablespoons juice |
| Limes, 1 medium | 2 tablespoons juice |
| Macaroni, spaghetti, and noodles, $^1/_2$ pound | 4 cups cooked |
| Milk, 1 quart | 4 cups |

| This Much... | Will Give You This... |
| --- | --- |
| Nuts: | |
| Peanuts, 5 ounces | 1 cup |
| Pecans, $4^1/_4$ ounces, chopped | 1 cup |
| Walnuts, $4^1/_2$ ounces, chopped | 1 cup |
| Oats, rolled, 1 pound | 5 cups |
| Onion, 1 medium, chopped | $^2/_3$ cup |
| Orange, 1 medium | About $^1/_2$ cup juice |
| Potatoes, 1 pound, unpeeled | 2 cups mashed |
| Rice, 1 cup uncooked | 3 cups cooked |
| Sugar, 1 pound | About 2 cups |
| Tomatoes, 1 pound | 3 medium |
| Yeast, $^1/_4$ ounce package | 1 scant tablespoon |

# Nutrition Information

## THE FOOD GUIDE PYRAMID

This Food Guide Pyramid is based on the U.S. Department of Agriculture and the U.S. Department of Health and Human Services dietary guidelines for Americans, which is intended to help people develop long-term healthy eating habits. Both the pyramid and the guidelines aim to provide ample essential nutrients and encourage minimal consumption of fat, saturated fat, cholesterol, and added sugars.

The foods at the base of the pyramid—breads, cereal, rice, and pasta—are excellent sources of vitamins, minerals, and fiber, are relatively low in fat and saturated fat, and are free of cholesterol.

Plant foods are rich in substances that some research indicates may be beneficial in controlling blood glucose levels, reducing blood cholesterol levels, controlling blood pressure, and protecting against certain diseases.

The Food Guide Pyramid suggests eating 6 to 11 servings per day from the bread, cereal, rice, and pasta group, and 3 to 5 servings from the fruit group. It recommends making food from these groups the focal point of most meals. Also suggested are 4 to 6 servings of dairy products and nuts, dried beans, and eggs. Fats, oil, and sweets, the top and the smallest portion of the pyramid, should be eaten sparingly.

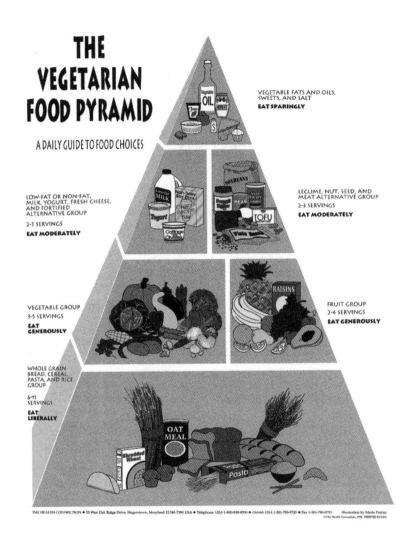

# THE VEGETARIAN FOOD PYRAMID

## A DAILY GUIDE TO FOOD CHOICES

VEGETABLE FATS AND OILS,
SWEETS, AND SALT
**EAT SPARINGLY**

LOW-FAT OR NON-FAT,
MILK, YOGURT, FRESH CHEESE,
AND FORTIFIED
ALTERNATIVE GROUP
2-3 SERVINGS
**EAT MODERATELY**

LEGUME, NUT, SEED, AND
MEAT ALTERNATIVE GROUP
2-3 SERVINGS
**EAT MODERATELY**

VEGETABLE GROUP
3-5 SERVINGS
**EAT
GENEROUSLY**

FRUIT GROUP
2-4 SERVINGS
**EAT GENEROUSLY**

WHOLE GRAIN
BREAD, CEREAL,
PASTA, AND RICE
GROUP
6-11
SERVINGS
**EAT
LIBERALLY**

THE HEALTH CONNECTION ◆ 55 West Oak Ridge Drive, Hagerstown, Maryland 21740-7390 USA ◆ Telephone: USA 1-800-548-8700 ◆ Outside USA 1-301-790-9735 ◆ Fax 1-301-790-9733    Illustration by Merle Poirier
© The Health Connection, 1994  PRINTED IN USA

## JUST WHAT IS A SERVING ANYWAY?

We've all seen it, that ambiguous "serving size suggestion" listed on the back of all the foods we buy...but what does it mean? Read on because these serving recommendations from the U.S. Department of Agriculture should help!

- **Bread, cereal, rice, and pasta:** 1 bread slice; 1 ounce ready-to-eat cereal; $1/2$ cup cooked cereal; $1/2$ cup cooked rice or pasta; 5 or 6 small crackers.

- **Vegetables:** 1 cup raw, leafy vegetables; $1/2$ cup cooked or chopped raw vegetables; $3/4$ cup vegetable juice.

- **Fruits:** 1 medium apple, banana, or orange; $1/2$ cup chopped, cooked, or canned fruit; $1/2$ cup dried fruit; $3/4$ cup fruit juice.

- **Milk, yogurt, and cheese:** 1 cup milk or yogurt; $1 1/2$ ounces natural cheese; 2 ounces processed cheese.

- **Dry beans, eggs, and nuts:** $1/2$ cup cooked, dry beans; 1 egg; 2 tablespoons peanut butter; $1/3$ cup nuts.

- **Fats, oils, and sweets:** No serving recommendation, except to use them sparingly.

# Where to Find What You're Looking For

# Now you can do these tasks, too!

## The Lazy Way

**S**tarting to think there are a few more of life's little tasks that you've been putting off? Don't worry—we've got you covered. Take a look at all of *The Lazy Way* books available. Just imagine—you can do almost anything *The Lazy Way!*

Handle Your Money The Lazy Way
By Sarah Young Fisher and Carol Turkington
0-02-862632-X

Build Your Financial Future The Lazy Way
By Terry Meany
0-02-862648-6

Cut Your Spending The Lazy Way
By Leslie Haggin
0-02-863002-5

Have Fun with Your Kids The Lazy Way
By Marilee Lebon
0-02-863166-8

Keep Your Kids Busy The Lazy Way
By Barbara Nielsen and Patrick Wallace
0-02-863013-0

Feed Your Kids Right The Lazy Way
By Virginia Van Vynckt
0-02-863001-7

*All Lazy Way books are just $12.95!

additional titles on the back!